HEAVEN

A COPTIC ORTHODOX CHRISTIAN PERSPECTIVE

Bishop Youannis

ST MARY & MOSES ABBEY PRESS

Heaven: A Coptic Orthodox Christian Perspective
By His Grace Bishop Youannis, of Gharbia, Egypt and its Suburbs

Copyright © 2021 Coptic Orthodox Diocese of the Southern U.S.A.

All rights reserved.

Designed & Published by:
St. Mary & St. Moses Abbey Press
101 S Vista Dr, Sandia, TX 78383
stmabbeypress.com

First Edition (Arabic): March 4, 1991. Anba Rouis' Church, Abbassia, Cairo, Egypt. Translated from Arabic by Margarite Rafla.

Library of Congress Control Number: 2019954003

Contents

Preface

Preface written in 2010, upon completion of the English translation of the book "Heaven," by His Grace Bishop Youannis, which was originally published in Arabic.

It brings us great pleasure to present to you the first English translation of the classic book, "Heaven" by His Grace Bishop Youannis, of blessed memory. We are thankful, first and foremost, to God for His blessing and help in permitting us to complete this work to the glory of His holy name.

We also wish to thank our beloved father, His Holiness Pope Shenouda III, for his blessing, prayers and invaluable encouragement. Last, but not least, we wish to thank all those who translated, typed, formatted, edited, proofread or otherwise sacrificed their time to offer their service toward the completion of this book. May the Lord reward each of them with the heavenly instead of the earthly and the eternal instead of the temporal.

The Old Testament references are taken from a modern version of Sir Thomas Brenton's English translation of the Septuagint, unless otherwise noted. The Psalms follow the Septuagint numbering as well. The New King James Version is included for New Testament references, unless otherwise noted. In a few places, English words appear in brackets. These are words that do not appear in the original text, but are necessary for clarification or serve as an alternative or addition.

We pray that God use this humble effort to the glory of His name and that He may bless our people in order that they may learn and comprehend the richness of heaven and eternal life through the intercessions of the Holy Theotokos, St. Mary, St. John the Evangelist, St. Mark the Apostle and Evangelist, and the prayers of His Holiness Pope Shenouda III.

His Grace Bishop Serapion

Bishop of the Coptic Orthodox Diocese of Los Angeles, Southern California, and Hawaii

His Grace Bishop Youssef

Bishop of the Coptic Orthodox Diocese of the Southern United States

Introduction

Heaven is the aim of all mankind. Our hearts long to attain it. We fervently hope to possess it. We struggle to reach it and be blessed by it. Contemplation on the glories of heaven and what awaits its saints gives those who struggle for it a spiritual push forward and makes them forget all their toils.

Although heaven is the aim of all mankind, not everyone will be blessed with its glories. To attain heaven and be blessed with its glories require basic principles of faith and spiritual qualifications. The Heavenly Jerusalem is the eternal bride for the Lamb whom He has purchased with His blood; He has shed His blood for the sake of all mankind. The Lord has prepared for the sojourners who have lived for Him and with Him in love and loyalty on earth, peaceful places in heaven. There, they will live with Him forever.

But what about heaven? Who has the right to be blessed by the eternal glory in heaven? Will God continue to be merciful as people know Him to be? Will He allow everyone, without any expectations, to enter heaven? And what will people do in heaven? Will the saints go straight to heaven after they leave their bodies? What happens after man dies? Will Christ truly come indeed a second time? What will He do?

The goal of this book is to answer all of these questions and others. The contents of this book were not originally intended to be printed in this form, but are the result of seven lectures preached during the Great Lent in Tanta and Mahala El Kobra in 1974. This book is published as these lectures were preached.

However, in order to explain the subject of heaven in all of its aspects, there will be a need for many other additions regarding this topic, which would need to be issued in a larger edition.

This book is the first of the books we will publish from the sermons given in the western diocese, where the Lord permitted me to be ordained as a servant and shepherd for it after six years. We look to the help provided for us from heaven above, so we may publish in sequence the fruit of our shepherding work during all of these years.

I am glad to present this first fruit to my sons and daughters, the Seminary students in Cairo and Tanta. This is an expression of my love and appreciation to them for their enthusiasm for learning. I ask God to make them knowledgeable servants, kindled by the Spirit, offering the Word of Truth to the people, and guiding them in the way of truth—the way to heaven and eternal glory.

I place this book in the hands of Him who loved us, and redeemed us, so it may be a source of blessing to all who read it.

May our blessed God, who called us to His eternal glory in Christ Jesus, kindle our hearts with His love. May He keep us all blameless and without obstacle until the time of His coming. To Him be all glory and honor to the end of ages, Amen.

March 19, 1978

10 Baramhat 1694 AM

Second Sunday of the Great Lent,

In Commemoration of the Glorious Feast of the Cross

Youannis,

By God's grace, the Bishop of Gharbia

1

Heaven and Us

God willing, this evening's topic is the beginning of a series about Heaven, which we shall speak upon during all of the Sundays of the Great Lent this year. Someone may ask why we chose the topic of heaven, and why this subject is so important.

Brethren, our entire life from beginning to end is linked to heaven now, afterwards and forever. It is linked to heaven now when we are in the physical state. Life is also linked to heaven after we leave the body, in this world and in eternity. Therefore, it is wise, reasonable and important for man to know something about heaven and his expansive, far-reaching labor to heaven after man leaves this body of dust.

Wisdom tells us to know the source we are dealing with and the place to which we are going. When one wishes to move from one house to another, they research the neighborhood conditions of the new home in which they plan to live. The same goes for an employee who is ordered to be relocated from one city to another. Likewise, when a person thinks about emigrating from one country to another, he begins to study the issues of this new country to which they will travel. They ask about the inhabitants, customs, weather patterns, etc. They read eagerly about it and studies all of its details.

If they study in great detail in this case, when their stay will be for a short period of time, then how much more should we be interested in knowing what concerns heaven?

With the grace of God, we shall tackle this evening the topic "Heaven and Us" from three aspects: man, the Lord Jesus and the purpose of heaven, as we discussed.

Man is a Heavenly Creature

Man is different than all the other creatures, for he is the only being who exists by the unity of the spirit and the body together. Without the body, man becomes complete spirit and would belong to the world of spirits. This is the destiny of those who go to the other world. Moreover, without the spirit, he does not become man. Rather, he is a mere body equal to an animal. We know that the body was created from dust, but the spirit was from God's breath.

This is why we constantly experience a contradiction between man's two elements: the spirit and the body. As an ultimate result of these dual components, there is a conflict between man's tendencies and desires. "For the flesh lusts against the Spirit, and the Spirit against the flesh" (Galatians 5:17). The Spirit is of heavenly essence, but the body's essence is of dust. These two essences are separated at death, but they are reunited in the general resurrection, after the body acquires new properties and remain like this forever. This will be explained in the fifth topic of our study, God willing.

We have come to know these facts in the story of creation, written by Moses the prophet in the Book of Genesis. "And God formed the man of the dust of the earth, and breathed into his nostrils the breath of life, and man became a living soul. And God planted a garden eastward in Eden, and He placed the man there whom He had formed...And the Lord God took the man whom He had formed, and placed him in the garden of Eden, to cultivate and keep it" (Genesis 2:7-8, 15). From these words, it is clear that man is a heavenly creature even though he was created from dust.

Heaven, to man, is the beginning and the end, the first and the last. It is his original homeland and his last dwelling. Man's beginning was the day he was created in heaven and it will be his end when he returns to it.

What is this dream that was declared to Jacob at Bethel: and the "ladder was fixed on the earth, whose top reached to heaven, and the angels of God ascended and descended on it. And the Lord stood upon it" (Genesis 28:12-13)? This is nothing other than the incarnation of man's existence and his relationship with heaven.

This fact has become absolutely clear in Christ's

personal image, our Savior, who told Nathaniel when he testified that He is the Son of God. "Most assuredly, I say to you, hereafter you shall see heaven open, and the angels of God ascending and descending upon the Son of Man" (John 1:51). The door of heaven was shut in man's face after the first disobedience. But it was opened once more before man's face by Christ's work of salvation, through His death, by which He reconciled man with God.

Man's Separation From God

Man is present on earth as a stranger for a certain period of time. The earth is not our country; we are only sojourners here. This deeply rooted feeling of estrangement exists in all mankind from the beginning. When Jacob, the father of fathers, stood before Pharaoh in Egypt and was asked, "How old are you?," he answered in recollection of the past, saying, "The days of the years of my life, wherein I sojourn, are one hundred and thirty years; few and evil have been the days of the years of my life, they have not attained to the days of the life of my fathers, in which days they sojourned" (Genesis 47:8-9).

The spiritually great David was often heard pleading before God in fear, humility and love, saying, "I am a stranger in the earth; do not hide Your commandments from me" (Psalms 118:19). He also says, "O Lord, listen to my prayer and my supplication; attend to my tears; be not silent, for I am a sojourner in the land, and a stranger, as all my fathers were" (Psalms 38:12). These are the men of God as expressed in the Old Testament.

When we turn to the New Testament, we find Saint Paul the Apostle confirming the issue of man's alien existence in the world throughout his epistles. In his epistle to the Hebrews, after he mentions a number of names of righteous people in the Old Testament, he says, "These all died in faith, not having received the promises, but having seen them afar off were assured of them, embraced them and confessed that they were strangers and pilgrims on the earth" (Hebrews 11:13). Moreover, he writes to the Corinthians, "So we are always confident, knowing that while we are at home in the body we are absent from the Lord. For we walk by faith, not by sight. We are confident, yes, well pleased rather, to be absent from the body and to be present with the Lord" (2 Corinthians 5:6-8).

Saint Peter the Apostle wrote his first epistle to "the pilgrims of the Dispersion in Pontus, Galatia, Cappadocia, Asia, and Bithynia" (1 Peter 1:1). He advises them saying, "Beloved, I beg you as sojourners and pilgrims, abstain from fleshly lusts which war against the soul" (1 Peter 2:11).

Our saintly forefathers struggled in showing the alien feeling we experience. This gave them strong motivation in their spiritual life. They lived in the flesh on earth as if they had no bodies, as spirits in heaven. Added to this is the deep, strong feeling of alienation that leads man to feel dead to the world and a tendency to a life of asceticism and seclusion, which puts distance between him and the iniquity of judging others. This clarifies the general expression that describes a religious person as someone who is "khein nifawy" which is often said as a joke or ridicule. This phrase in the Coptic language is "khen nifawy" meaning "from heaven" or "heavenly"! I wish we could all be "khein nifawy." This is an all-inclusive expression relating to our forefathers, the saints.

Man's Contract With Heaven

Since man is a heavenly creature, he is constantly in contract should this instead be contact? with heaven. This undoubtedly springs from his hope in heaven, which makes Saint Paul say, "We give thanks to the God and Father of our Lord Jesus Christ, praying always for you, since we heard of your faith in Christ Jesus and of your love for all the saints; because of the hope which is laid up for you in heaven" (Colossians 1:3-5). This constant touch is demonstrated in five points: eagerness for heaven, the prayers, the offerings, the intercession of the angels and saints, and prayer for the departed.

1. Eagerness for Heaven

Heaven, as an idea, is not unusual to man—even if he does not express it with his own tongue—for it is deeply rooted within him and constantly attracts him. This is what urged Saint Paul to say, "For our citizenship is in heaven, from which we also eagerly wait for the Savior, the Lord Jesus Christ" (Philippians 3:20). On another occasion, he urges the believers, saying, "If then you were raised with Christ, seek those things which are above, where Christ is, sitting at the right hand of God. Set your mind on things above, not on things on the earth" (Colossians 3:1-2). David the Prophet, the righteous man of prayer, tells God how his heart is longing for Him: "As the deer earnestly desires the fountains of water, so my soul earnestly longs for You, O God. My soul has thirsted for the living God; when shall I come and appear before God?" (Psalms 41:1-2). What a hopeful expression this is, "When shall I come and appear before God?" When shall I see you, O God, and meet You and stand in Your presence?

Man, by his nature and his emotions, is in heaven. We need to understand our Christianity by the spirit, and not by our minds—for our spirits are able to embrace, touch and even kiss God. "Let Him kiss me with the kisses of His mouth" (Song 1:2).

This longing is well-rooted in man's heart. This is what explains the adoration of the saints and their tremendous love for our Lord and Savior, Jesus Christ. An example of this love is when we hear about someone who deserted the world, went to one of the monasteries and secluded himself in a cave.

At this point, some doubtful people who are far away from the correct faith begin to make fun of such an attitude and say scornfully that too much prayer causes madness! But such people are poor, indeed, because their hearts have not experienced the deep true love towards our Lord, and the inward longing for Him. Therefore, they are unable to realize the depth of the spiritual motives that have compelled those who loved God more than themselves to depart from the world and all that it is therein. Consequently, they can find no reason or explanation for this ascetic life.

Imagine the longing feeling of a mother for her traveling daughter. Imagine the father's longing for his distant children. These parents perpetually repeat how much they miss and long for their children.

If this is the case with human love at its best image, then why do we doubt the most sublime love, which is that of the saints towards God, and their longing for Him?

2. Prayers

Prayers are an expression of man's love and longing for God. Through prayers, we turn to the living God in heaven. To Him we pour out our complaints, our worries and our troubles. We admit before Him our weaknesses and we offer Him our love. We express our adoration of Him and we uncover our sorrows and our eagerness for Him.

The Holy Book introduces prayer to us as a great support in man's sojourn on earth. The Lord Jesus, as well as the saints, spoke much about prayer. All the saints and the men of God turned to heaven in prayer, "To You, I have lifted up my eyes, You who dwells in heaven." How overwhelming is Christ's analogy of the eternal glory that awaits the believers! They are invited to a wedding in the parable of the ten virgins (Matthew 25). Saint Paul the Apostle tells the faithful, "For I am jealous for you with godly jealousy. For I have betrothed you to one husband, that I may present you as a chaste virgin to Christ" (2 Corinthians 11:2) Where is this one Groom to whom our souls are engaged? He is in heaven!

3. Charity and Offerings

In Christianity, charity and offerings confirm the fact that man is a heavenly creature. Christ, to Him be all the glory, said, "Do not lay up for yourselves treasures on earth, where moth and rust destroy and where thieves break in and steal; but lay up for yourselves treasures in heaven, where neither moth nor rust destroys and where thieves do not break in and steal" (Matthew 6:19-20). This means that in heaven, we have a personal savings account in the greatest and biggest bank. There, we have our deposits kept, with interest and money-making. It is a secure bank, because Christ is the Trustee of the bank.

Therefore, we have to deposit our treasures in heaven's bank. In this way, the Lord Jesus assures us with His words that man is a heavenly creature who stands on earth but whose hands can reach the heavens. Thus he should invest his money in a savings account in heaven. This account has a key in the hand of every client in the bank. Thus, we find the Lord Jesus urging us to help our needy brethren, as in the parable of the unjust steward: "And I say to you, make friends for yourselves by unrighteous mammon, that when you fail, they may receive you into an everlasting home" (Luke 16:9). All of this confirms the amazing link between man and heaven. Anyone who gives charity to someone in need is someone who touches heaven with his hand while he is still on earth.

4. Intercession of the Angels and Saints and Prayer for the Departed

We do not wish in this respect to go into written proofs of the creed that confirms intercession and its effect. We shall not probe into this subject from this angle. Every day, we see and hear of miracles that happen in honor of the martyrs and saints. This is not surprising, since there is a general partnership between the living on earth and the departed in heaven, foremost with the saints and martyrs—an absolutely perfect partnership. We plead for their intercession and we contact them in different ways. As a result, we obtain their help for us.

A professor of philosophy from an American university, who was also a leader of a large religious group, came to visit the monasteries at Wadi El Natroun a few years ago. I happened to escort him on one of his visits. He admired the peaceful life the desert monks lived. Then, all of a sudden, he asked me if we had a telephone at the monastery. I answered, "Yes, we only have a telephone that contacts heaven directly." He was very pleased with this answer. After returning to America, he sent me a letter in which he recorded his admiration of the life of seclusion in the wilderness. He did not forget to record his memories of the wonderful and amazing telephone that contacts heaven directly!

Contacting heaven and its inhabitants is very easy and possible. You just have to call the saint, "O Virgin Mary, Mother of Light; O Archangel Michael; O Saint George; O Saint Mina, etc." Immediately, our call reaches their ears, and they quickly come to our rescue. If we could tolerate to see their bright heavenly appearance without fear, we would have seen them with our physical eyes. But it is due to our Lord's compassion that He hides their appearance from us, for He knows our weakness, and our inability to see that which is heavenly. If we had the ability to see the angels and those in heaven fearlessly, and without any adverse effect, God would have allowed us to see them.

Our Orthodox Church asks for the intercession of the saints and believes in its unconditional power. This is obvious in the church's various prayers, especially in its praises. In the Matins Doxology that is said before the Morning Offering of Incense, we offer the gift of praise to each of the saints by name, as if we are telling them, "Good morning, O Virgin, Mother of Light... Good morning Archangel Michael...Good morning Saint Antony..., etc." In this way we constantly live with the inhabitants in heaven. We call them and are always in contact with them.

The late Deacon Mikhail Girgis, the chanter in the church of Saint Mark, related to me the following story. He said, "One day I was praying in Saint Mark's Church in Klout Bey Street in Cairo. I was still young at this time. As I was chanting the praise alone, I felt there were people with me sharing in the offering of praise. I became conscious of this and asked those around me who was sharing in the chanting. They answered, 'No one, teacher.' So I felt the saints were the ones offering the praise with me."

There was another chanter in the Saint George the Martyr Church in a small village in Lower Egypt. While he was chanting the praise alone in the church, he had a vision of Saint George dancing on his horse in the heart of the church with the hymns accompanying him. Thus, there is a dynamic relationship between us and those in heaven.

This is why the Church expresses this concept in the Commemoration of the Saints in every liturgy, saying, "As this, O Lord, is the command of Your only-begotten Son, that we share in the commemoration of Your saints, graciously accord, O Lord, to remember all the saints who have pleased You since the beginning..." Then the names of many of those saints are mentioned. You also pray and say, "Those O Lord, whose souls You have taken, repose them in the paradise of joy..." In the Liturgy of Saint Cyril, there is an amazingly sweet feeling of this shared relationship. In great humility, the priest says after the commemoration, "Not that we are worthy, O our Master, of the intercession for the blessedness of those saints, but rather they are standing before the throne of Your only-begotten Son, that they may be in our stead, interceding for our poverty and our frailty. May You be a forgiver of our iniquities, for the sake of their holy prayers and for the sake of Your holy name which is called upon us."

The Church continually prays for the saints who dwell in heaven, in appreciation of the effort they exerted for the Church and the Christian faith. It is also a declaration and confirmation of the existing relationship between those on earth and those who have departed to heaven.

Man Has the Authority in Heaven

Because man is a heavenly creature, he has authority in heaven. This authority is different than that of priesthood. Can you imagine, dear brethren, that man, while he is still on earth, has the authority in heaven? This authority is given to every real believer. For Joshua, the son of Nun and the successor of Moses the prophet, in leading the people, managed to stop the sun in heaven! Thus the sun did not set for almost an entire day (Joshua 10:12-13). Elijah the prophet managed to shut the sky so it did not rain for three and a half years. He prayed and then it opened again (1 Kings 17:1; Job 5:17-18). This authority is definite proof that man is a heavenly creature; otherwise he would not have had the authority over heaven.

As for the priests, Christ gave them the unique authority to loose and to bind in heaven and on earth. Christ gave this authority to the saintly disciples for their mission and service saying, "And I will give you the keys of the kingdom of heaven, and whatever you bind on earth will be bound in heaven, and whatever you loose on earth will be loosed in heaven" (Matthew 16:19). It is evident that this command was not for Saint Peter alone, but it was for all of the apostles. In any situation, the apostles also are human. If the Lord Jesus has given them the keys of the heavenly kingdom and has equipped them with this authority, then this is absolute proof that man is a heavenly creature.

God's Houses on Earth

Let us meditate on this great mystery, as to how God, who dwells in heaven, has chosen for Himself a dwelling place on earth. This began when God said to Moses the prophet, "And you [the Sons of Israel] shall make Me a sanctuary, and I will appear among you" (Exodus 25:8) The tabernacle and the temple were the two places where God dwelt among the sons of Israel.

The Lord Jesus assured us of this meaning when He drove out the sellers from the temple, saying, "My house shall be called a house of prayer for all nations" (Mark 11:17). Saint Paul the Apostle also confirms the same meaning when he told his disciple Timothy, "These things I write to you, though I hope to come to you shortly, but if I am delayed, I write so that you may know how you ought to conduct yourself in the house of God, which is the church of the living God, the pillar and ground of the truth" (1 Timothy 3:14-15). For the church is the house of God. Just as God dwells in the heaven above, likewise does He dwell here on earth in the church where man meets Him.

Heaven Is the Last Dwelling for Man

One of the most significant indications that man is a heavenly creature is that if a man began his life in heaven when he was created, then he will eventually end there. This reality has been declared and unfolded by many expressions, statements and divine words in the Holy Book, God's message to mankind. The Lord Jesus, in His memorable Sermon on the Mount, when He was blessing those who would be persecuted for His sake, said, "Rejoice and be exceedingly glad, for great is your reward in heaven" (Matthew 5:11-12). If we tackle a personality such as Saint Paul the Apostle, for instance, we find him portraying this point. He says, "For we know that if our earthly house, this tent, is destroyed, we have a building from God, a house not made with hands, eternal in the heavens. For in this we groan, earnestly desiring to be clothed with our habitation which is from heaven" (2 Corinthians 5:1-2). In his epistle to the Hebrews, after mentioning some of the righteous in the Old Testament and how they were aliens to the world, he says, "But now they desire a better, that is, a heavenly country" (Hebrews 11:16). When Saint Paul speaks of the resurrection of the departed, he says "And as we have borne the image of the man of dust, we shall also bear the image of the heavenly Man" (1 Corinthians 15:49).

Finally, when this great apostle felt death was drawing near, he wrote to his disciple Timothy saying, "And the Lord will deliver me from every evil work and preserve me for His heavenly kingdom" (2 Timothy 4:18). The Holy Book is full of verses that demonstrate that our end is in heaven. This fact confirms without any doubt that man is a creature of heaven. For this reason, man is so concerned with all that pertains to heaven. He knows for sure that this is his eventual destiny. Thus he is tied to it in his lifetime and also after his death.

Saint Gregory the Theologian of Nazianzus says, "When I witness the overwhelming joy that man gains by dying and the triviality of what he loses by departing from life, I cannot bear any eagerness so intense to go up to heaven. I cry out to God saying, 'When, O God, will You deliver me from this life and make me dwell in my dear country?'"

The Lord Jesus' Teaching About Man and Heaven

The one who meditates on the Holy Gospels finds them full of many expressions mentioned by the Lord of Glory that testify of man's fundamental relationship with heaven. This is not surprising because the Lord Jesus was the first to link man to God in a clearly strong image that speaks of love and a firm foundation. The Lord Jesus called himself "Son of Man," or the "Son of mankind," whereas He called humans, "sons of God." In other words, He has made God Father to mankind. This is a direct fruit of the mystery of the Divine Incarnation.

Our Church expresses this in the annual Friday Theotokia. The praise says about Christ, "He took what is ours and gave us what is His, we praise and glorify Him, and exalt Him." He took what is ours, that is, the body. He gave us what is His, that is, our sharing with Him His godly nature (2 Peter 1:4). Christ loved to use the words, "heavenly Father," "your heavenly Father," and "your Father who is in heaven." This is, no doubt, an expression of the strong link between us and God. It also discerns the earthly physical fatherhood. The Lord Jesus when He said, "Do not call anyone on earth your father" (Matthew 23:9), was likely implying our link to the heavenly Father as our Supporter.

Christ often spoke of this heavenly fatherhood: "For if you forgive men their trespasses, your heavenly Father will also forgive you" (Matthew 6:14). And again "Look at the birds of the air, for they neither sow nor reap nor gather into barns; yet your heavenly Father feeds them. Are you not of more value than they?" (Matthew 6:26). He also emphasizes the necessity of our relying on the heavenly Father in all of our physical needs when He says, "For after all these things the Gentiles seek. For your heavenly Father knows that you need all these things" (Matthew 6:32). Therefore, we can say that man in Christianity is transformed from a physical person to another one who knows, in Christ, his real self and his real nature—that he is a heavenly creature.

Contemplate on this amazing radical change that has sprung up from Christianity! For before Christ's coming, the entire humanity believed themselves to be merely God's slaves. But in Christ we have become sons and heirs, and even heirs of God with Christ (Galatians 4:7). Without question, this is a deep, radical change! Do not think Christianity is only a mission for edification. Christianity has made a deep radical change that is not restricted merely to words, but surpasses this and reaches the essence.

As proof of this, Christ taught us when we pray to cry out, "Our Father who art in heaven" (Matthew 6:9). This sonship to God is not a matter of honor or social dignity only, but it is sonship on an actual level. This is obtained by man in his second birth which is blessed baptism (John 3:3-13). Christ has two births: the first is before the ages, "born of the Father before all ages;" the second one is limited. Likewise, man also has two births. Christ has come for our salvation and has blessed our nature by uniting God's divinity with humanity, which Christ has taken from the chaste Virgin Mary. He too has come to have two births: a physical birth by natural delivery and a second birth from God and the Church which is of the water and the Spirit, by means of the holy baptism.

The Lord Jesus, glory be to Him, has manifested to us man's relationship with heaven by means of beautiful parables concerning the heavenly kingdom mentioned by Saint Matthew the Evangelist in Chapter 13. These are the parables of the sower, the wheat and the tares; the mustard seed; the leaven hidden by the woman in the measures of flour; the hidden treasure in the field; and the net thrown out in the sea. These parables manifest man's relationship when on earth with heaven.

The Present Life Is the Preparation for Life in Heaven

Finally, dear brethren, let us understand the wisdom concerning why we have come into the world. It is a phase of sojourning, where we are trained just as God trained His people for forty years in the wilderness before they set foot in the Promised Land. There many similarities between this phase and man's estrangement on earth, until he reaches the heavenly Jerusalem, the hope of all the faithful. The earthly Jerusalem was only a symbol and a portrayal of it. It is a period in which we draw our eternal future. While on earth, we build the house which will be ours when we enter heaven. We build it with our life, our deeds, our attitude and our strife. Therefore, what do we have to do and what kind of life is it of which we will be worthy to attain this eternal and great glory? This is what we shall tackle in the forthcoming chapters.

2

Heaven is a Confirmed Fact and Reality

The Meaning of the Word "Heaven"

Before we discuss today's subject, we must answer one question: What is the meaning of "heaven"? The word, "heaven" has been used to describe the sublime world above in the universe that God has created, as opposed to the earth, the lower part dedicated to human dwelling. While earth is the human dwelling for sinners and was cursed due to man's sin, heaven is a special place, a sanctified place, in which God manifests Himself for His creation.

The word "heaven" in the Arabic language is derived from "sublime"—that is, to be exalted and elevated. It is heaven alone that is above us. The exact same meaning is found in other languages as well. In English, heaven means "heaved up" in its original derivation. The word "heaven" in the ancient languages has the same meaning. In Greek it is *ouranos*, in Hebrew, *shaamayim*, a word close to the Arabic one, since the Hebrew and Arabic languages have the same linguistic origin.

The Jews believe, as is evident in their writings, that there are three heavens. The first heaven is meant to be the space enveloping the earth (the atmosphere). The second heaven is the frost where the stars and the planets are situated (outer-space). As for the third heaven, they call it the heaven of heavens, where God's throne is, as well as the angelic spirits and the dwellings of the saints.

It is agreed the heaven mentioned in our Church's creed ("He ascended into heaven") is not the first and second heavens, as the Jews believe. For us, the first heaven is the space enveloping the earth, which Saint Basil the Great calls, the "bird's heaven." The second heaven is the frost and ice where the stars and planets are located. As for the third heaven, this is different than that of the Jews. Our Church believes that the third heaven is Paradise. This is clear from the words of Saint Paul the Apostle: "I know a man in Christ who fourteen years ago—whether in the body I do not know, or whether out of the body I do not know, God knows—such a one was caught up to the third heaven. And I know such a man—whether in the body or out of the body I do not know, God knows—how he was caught up into Paradise and heard inexpressible words, which it is not lawful for a man to utter" (2 Corinthians 12:2-4). It is from here that the Creed of our Church came to be, that the third heaven is Paradise.

In other words, it is the place where the righteous souls await. The saints who depart from this world go to the third heaven and stay there until the general judgment. It is the place where the souls of the righteous who departed stay and wait. This differs from the place where the wicked stay, which is fiery hell or the abyss. By the will of God, we shall later discuss this subject in detail.

Despite the absolute belief that God is present everywhere, the Holy Book constantly describes God to be present in a higher place that is more glorious, which is heaven. For instance, in Genesis 17:22, we read "Then He left off speaking with him, and God went up from Abraham." The words "went up," means ascended to a higher place, which is heaven. In the story of the inauguration of the temple built by Solomon, the son of David, it is said, "And Solomon stood up in front of the altar before all the congregation of Israel; and he spread out his hands toward heaven, and he said: 'Lord God of Israel, there is no God like You in heaven above and on the earth below, keeping covenant and mercy with Your servant who walks before You with all his heart; ... And You shall hearken to the prayer of Your servant, and of Your people Israel, which they shall pray toward this place; And you shall hear in Your dwelling place in heaven, and You shall do and be gracious'" (1 Kings 8:22-23, 30). The Lord Jesus, glory be to Him, when speaking to Nicodemus, says, "No one has ascended to heaven but He who came down from heaven, that is, the Son of Man who is in heaven" (John 3:13). In this way, despite the belief that Gods' presence is everywhere, He is always described as being in a certain place we call "heaven." Therefore, the Lord Jesus, glory be to Him, told His disciples when some of them could not understand His words about Him giving them His body, "What then if you should see the Son of Man ascend where He was before?" (John 6:62). Moreover, on the dawn of His glorious resurrection, He told Mary Magdalene, "Do not cling to Me, for I have not yet ascended to My Father; but go to My brethren and say to them, 'I am ascending to My Father and your Father, and to My God and your God'" (John 20:17). In Saint Luke's gospel, he recorded about the Lord's ascension: "Now when He had spoken these things, while they watched, He was taken up, and a cloud received Him out of their sight. And while they looked steadfastly toward heaven as He went up, behold, two men stood by them in white apparel, who also said, "Men of Galilee, why do you stand gazing up into heaven? This same Jesus, who was taken up from you into heaven, will so come in like manner as you saw Him go into heaven" (Acts 1:9-11).

As for Saint Paul the Apostle, when speaking of the faith, he says, "Do not say in your heart, 'Who will ascend into heaven?' (that is, to bring Christ down from above)" (Romans 10:6).

The Evidence About the Reality of Heaven

Someone may ask, "How can I be sure that a heaven like this really exists?" We answer him that heaven is an assured reality. We now present five proofs that confirm the existence of this reality:

1. The Testimony of Life and Your Existence.

Your being or existence is the subconscious feeling or primitive instinct that exists deep in the human soul. Man alone has this unique instinct among all the other creatures living on earth. Man's belief in a god or an afterlife and his faith in the concept of immortality is an instinctive feeling declared by mankind—from the ancient times until today. Those who declared this were from various cultures, levels and races and during every time and place. This feeling has been declared by everyone, beginning with the Eskimos—the inhabitants of the iced climate in the extreme northern part of the globe—to those who live in the unknown, equatorial forests and jungles in Africa. This primitive and instinctive feeling could weaken within some people at certain times, according to certain circumstances. But it is never completely eliminated, for it soon awakens again and is renewed.

This instinctive feeling in man is worthy of further study. People in all generations believe in the concept of an afterlife and in immortality. This belief is found in atheism, and has appeared since the dawn of history, ever since man came to exist on the face of this earthly planet. There is a deeply scientific study performed by a famous French scientist in the nineteenth century, Fustel de Coularges, which has been compiled in a valuable publication called, "The Antique City" ("La Cite Antique"). It contains contemporary research about the worship, laws and doctrines of the Greeks and Romans. I was amazed at the references and documentation referred to by this brilliant scholar. He says,

> No matter how much we speak about the Indo-European race, of which the Greek and the Romans are derived, we discover that this race has never believed that everything would come to an end for man after this short life. The oldest generation, long before any philosophers came to be, they thought about the afterlife succeeding this one. They did not face death for its disintegration of humans, but because it was an easy alteration for life. The burial rituals clearly demonstrate that when they laid the body in the grave, they believed at the same time they buried something alive. At the end of the funeral ceremony, it was their custom was to call on the spirit of the departed by shouting his name three times. They wished him a happy life in his burial, saying three times, "Be healthy" and adding, "May the burial be easy upon you." It was to this extent that they believed the being would continue to live under the earth and that he continue to experience happiness and pain. They used to write on the tombstone that the person is restful there.

Thus we can see that the primitive people had the inner belief that man would be immortalized in another world. At this point, we may ask, "Who brought about this instinctive feeling in humans?" Surely, this feeling could not possibly be created by man and spread across all people of different races and cultures.

The belief of the ancient Pharaohs of Egypt in immortality and the afterlife was much deeper and far greater. This concept of immortality and the afterlife dominated their thinking. So, they made mummies of their dead and bade the dead farewell with anthems full of hopeful words. Due to this belief, they built the tombs, temples and pyramids for their funeral rites. The engravings on these monuments still exist today and demonstrate the deeply rooted concept of immortality and their firm belief in the afterlife. It is a fact that the world's museums still posses many of these ancient Egyptian mummies. We have also discovered many of the prayers and hopeful songs that they sung for their dead. Much of today's lamentation and funeral rituals are rooted in those of the Egyptian Pharaohs.

The memorable artifacts built by our Egyptian forefathers related to death and immortality. They constructed gigantic tombs such as the pyramids and the kings' graves which they carved in the rocks, so they could preserve their dead until their return to life. They have also left us many of their funeral temples. The ancient Egyptians did not forget to record to us on their temples and tombs, their doctrine concerning death and immortality. We also must mention what is known as the "Book of the Dead."

The pyramids and the kings' tombs are not the only evidence for the belief in the afterlife. Rather, the Egyptians believed in the resurrection and the immortality of the dead since the beginning of time. Scientists have discovered in Beni Salama tombs dating back to the dawn of civilization. They discovered that the Egyptians used to bury their dead at this very early time in their history in a squatting position, with their knees close to their chin—which is the same position of an embryo while in his/her mother's womb. This is a strong image of the resurrection—that man will come to life a second time just as when emerging out of his mother's womb in his physical birth.

When Plutarch, the Greek historian and atheist (1st century BC until the 1st century AD), noticed this general religious feeling among the people, he said, "If you go around the entire world, you might find cities having no currency or schools or theaters. But up until now, no one has seen a city without a temple for worship or prayer." The well-known Roman philosopher, Seneca (1st century AD) adds to these words, saying, "When all people agree on one thing, then this is enough evidence of it being correct, such as in the existence of gods, for instance. All mankind agree about this."

As a result of all this evidence, we conclude that the belief in the existence of heaven and the afterlife is based on a well-founded fact. People at all times and places would not have believed in life after death if there had not been a spiritual and primitive feeling for such an assumption.

This is a godly instinct that God has inserted in man, just as with all other instincts. God did not put this instinct in man to make fun of him. For God created eyes in man in order for him to see with them the light. He made ears for him so he would hear with them. Likewise, this instinct was not placed in man for no reason! Concerning this, the

French philosopher, Rene Descartes (17th century AD), says, "Though I have this feeling of personal inferiority, I feel at the same time the presence of an absolutely entire self. I feel I am obliged to believe that this feeling I have inserted in myself, by this absolute self, is God."

2. The Obvious Reality of Heaven

Some of those who deny the concept of immortality and life after death believe, either due to ignorance or self-will, that there is no heaven, paradise or eternal agony. They want to live in iniquity and remain close to evil. By doing so, they try to settle their conscience by assuming that there is neither heaven nor hell, and no punishment or reward.

We have numerous examples of this approach. He who does not wish to fast, proclaims fasting is unlawful. He who avoids confession before a priest contradicts the existence of the sacrament of confession, a position which is not supported by the Holy Gospel. Therefore, most of those who deny the presence of heaven, paradise and punishment, do so willfully and meaningfully.

If we believe that God is both merciful and just, then we must also believe that those who have toiled here on earth will rest in heaven, and those who suffered in the world will be rewarded in heaven. On the other hand, we still feel the impact of the punishment imposed on man for his disobedience that is mentioned in the book of Genesis until this very day! God told Eve that she would conceive and give birth in pain and toil, and to this day every woman feels these pains in her pregnancy and delivery. (Genesis 3:16). Likewise, God's judgment and condemnation of Adam still remains to this day, for man still labors and sweats to eat his bread and the thistles and thorns still grow from the ground (Genesis 3:17–19). Therefore, this is obvious proof about God's words mentioned in the book of Genesis. If this is the case, then why do we not yield to God's word about heaven, eternity, reward and punishment?

A wonderful story reveals this message:

> There was a man who lived in a tent in the desert. Some scientists used to go to this desert in search of monuments. When they reached this man's tent, they heard him praying inside the tent and waited until he finished his prayers. Then they came forward to meet him.
>
> They told him, mockingly, "How do you know for sure there is a god who answers your prayers?"
>
> He answered them, saying, "How did you know that a man visited me in my tent last night?" They responded, "We came to know this by means of his footprints in the sand."
>
> He said, "I, too, know there is a God because I can see His prints everywhere."

Yes, God leaves His traces around us in everything and in everyplace. Has the Lord Jesus not said, "Heaven is My throne, and the earth is My footstool"? (Isaiah 66:1). It is as if God is walking on the earth among mankind, leaving behind various prints and traces. Nature proves in its laws that 'matter is never destroyed.' For instance, if we burn a piece of wood, it turns into ashes. But it does not lose its existence. All of the elements that compose this piece of wood have taken another form—ashes and gases. But none of it has been wiped out of existence. If solid materials, such as pieces of wood, are not wiped out, but only change in apparent shape, then can this not happen also with man, who is regarded as the most impressive of all creatures? Is this not the teaching of the Holy Book about God, "Who will transform our lowly body that it may be conformed to His glorious body, according to the working by which He is able even to subdue all things to Himself" (Philippians 3:21)? Saint Paul also says, "Behold, I tell you a mystery: We shall not all sleep, but we shall all be changed—in a moment, in the twinkling of an eye, at the last trumpet. For the trumpet will sound, and the dead will be raised incorruptible, and we shall be changed" (1 Corinthians 15:51–52).

3. Nature's Testimony that Heaven Really Exists

Contemplation on Nature Proves Heaven's Existence

Nature is the first and oldest witness of heaven, God's presence, and the existence of another life in heaven. It is enough only to lift your eyes to shout with David, saying, "The heavens declare the glory of God; and the firmament proclaims the work of His hands" (Psalms 18:1). We also cry out with our teacher, Saint Paul the

Apostle, saying, "For since the creation of the world His invisible attributes are clearly seen, being understood by the things that are made, even His eternal power and Godhead, so that they are without excuse" (Romans 1:20).

Nature, when contemplated, turns into a great place of worship where we meditate on God's greatness and His power. This is what prompted one of the philosophers to say, "The universe is the book of divinity read by the philosophers. To them, it was a Bible. It is God's mirror in which they saw His most beautiful image. It is the trumpet that proclaims God's plan, with all He made in its systematic discipline."

Newton, the British scholar of physics (1642–1727) said, "I have seen God in the works of nature and its laws. These prove that the existence of wisdom and power are not materialistic." Moreover, one of the great thinkers wrote, when meditating upon nature, "God's majesty is clearly manifested in everything: in the sun, the moon, the stars, and in all of nature."

The Son of God has formed all of creation for this great purpose, so He manifests through it His glories and greatness. When we enjoy the parks or the breeze, we can feel His kindness, His sweetness and His tender presence. When we see the blooming flower or the lilies covered in white snow, we can see His love, His chastity and His purity. The overflowing crystal streams are none other than the expression of His compassion, His grace and His beauty! The shining sun, the golden horizon and the beautiful rainbow glittering in the sky are nothing more than some shades of His glory and His goodness. Because of this, Christ has been called the "Sun of Righteousness"

(Malachi 4:2), the "Morning Star" (Revelations 2:28; 22:16), "the Apple among the trees of the wood" (Song 2:3), and "a gazelle or a young hart" (Song 2:9).

Living Creatures Also Prove the Existence of Heaven

In nature, we are able to see numerous proofs about the presence of the Great Creator. Take the example of the silk-worm. In autumn, it is secluded maybe under the leaf of a fig tree. It then covers itself with a delicate, silky fabric and quickly thickens and congeals until it becomes a "cocoon." Thus, the silk worm is isolated, removed from all eyes or inspection. So some might even think it has died and no longer exists. But this is not true. As soon as the spring draws near and nature begins to burst to life, the cocoon opens automatically. A butterfly emerges out of it and flies over the branches, across the fields, to begin again the cycle of life after we had assumed it was dead. Is not this life after death?

The Trees in Autumn. In autumn, the leaves of the trees fall and nothing is left more than the trunks and the branches. The observer might imagine that the trees have died in wintertime, especially in the cold regions where the snow covers the trees with a layer of sleet. But as soon as spring emerges, the snow melts, and life beats once more in the trees, and they begin to sprout new leaves. In no time, they blossom and become fruitful. In this way we feel and touch nature in trees after they had been covered with the garment of death.

The Plants. If we move on to other plants, such as

the crops of the field, we discover that the seeds do not sprout unless they are buried in the soil. After they are watered, they grow, blossom and are fruitful. The Lord Jesus, glory be to Him, confirmed this meaning, when He said, "Most assuredly, I say to you, unless a grain of wheat falls into the ground and dies, it remains alone; but if it dies, it produces much grain" (John 12:24). This is exactly what happens to man. He dies and is buried. But soon enough, he appears and blossoms in heaven after a short or long time. In this way we can see that nature is an honest witness of the existence of heaven.

4. The Arguments of Atheists

It is amazing that we base the evidence of heaven's existence on the words of atheists who deny the presence of God, heaven and life after death—even though there are proofs that confirm these concepts. These atheists are scientists and philosophers and have achieved great fame in the field of science and thinking. Yet, despite all of this, they are ignorant in the eyes of God. Divine inspiration describes them as being foolish, "The fool has said in his heart, 'There is no God'" (Psalms 13:1). Saint Paul the Apostle mentions the same thing in a different way when he says, "For the wisdom of this world is foolishness with God" (1 Corinthians 3:19). Job was right when he said, "But ask now the beasts, if they may speak to you, and the birds of the air, if they may declare to you. Tell the earth, if it may speak to you, and the fish of the sea shall explain to you. Who then has not known in all these things, that the hand of the Lord has made them? Seeing that the life of all living things is in His hand, and the breath of every man" (Job 12:7–10).

What is amazing is that despite the apparent atheism that some try to hide in—trying to forget God's presence and the life in heaven—for some reason or another, we find many of them becoming very weak at the moment of death. They express what they fear and are worried about the dark future that awaits them. Some of these atheists include the famous Thomas Hobbs who said at the moment of his death, "I am taking a dreadful jump into darkness!"

Mirabeau, one of the leaders of the great French Revolution (1789), said on his deathbed at the moment of his departure, "Give me more heroin so I can be unconscious, because I do not want to think of eternal life."

Charles IX, the ruthless dictator, said during his death, "I do not know where I am, I am lost forever. I know this very well."

Therefore, we should not be surprised if we realize that many of those who denied the faith in their youth, when they had strength, authority and intelligence, returned to themselves in their last days. They admitted their denial particularly of God and eternal life in heaven.

Among such people is Napoleon Bonaparte, who after living in exile on Saint Helen's Island, returned to himself. The French philosopher Voltaire, the American physicist Thomas Edison, the Russian writer and philosopher Tolstoy, and many others all returned to admit the immeasurable power of God.

If we compare their deaths to the saints, we see how the latter amazingly accepted death so joyfully. The heroic martyrs raced towards death, facing it in aspiration, with a smile on their lips—as if approaching a date of encounter with someone for whom they have been longing.

To prove this, it is enough to remember the wonderful words with which Saint John the Apostle concludes his book of Revelation and the entire Holy Bible: "Amen. Even so, come, Lord Jesus!" (Revelations 22:20). How great is the difference between those martyrs and saints and the atheists who were terrified and traumatized when they felt themselves approaching eternity!

5. God's Words and Declarations Concerning Heaven

Some may think that what is said about heaven is only mere imagination. But when we read His Holy Book, we if God speaking to us much about it. "All Scripture is given by inspiration of God, and is profitable for doctrine, for reproof, for correction, for instruction in righteousness, that the man of God may be complete, thoroughly equipped for every good work" (2 Timothy 3:16–17). This is why we believe what has been told to us about heaven, for we could not possibly have come to know these things except by means of divine inspiration. For no one knows anything about heaven except God Himself. Therefore, if we want to know the real heaven, we should resort to God's Word. Now we will mention some examples of God's words in His Holy Book.

In the second of the ten commandments, the Lord said, "You shall not make for yourself an idol, nor likeness of anything, whatever things are in the heaven above, and whatever are in the earth beneath, and whatever are in the waters under the earth" (Exodus 20:4). David the prophet said, "Now I know that the LORD has saved His Christ; He shall hear Him from His holy heaven: the salvation of His right hand is mighty" (Psalms 19:6); "The LORD is in His holy temple; as for the Lord, His throne is in heaven: His eyes look upon the poor, His eyelids test the sons of men" (Psalms 10:5); "He who dwells in the heavens shall laugh them to scorn, and the LORD shall mock them" (Psalms 2:4); and "The LORD has prepared His throne in the heaven; and His kingdom rules over all" (Psalms 102:19).

The wise Solomon, after he built the temple, said, "But will God indeed dwell with men upon the earth? If the heaven and heaven of heavens will not suffice You, how much less even this house which I have built for Your name?" (1 Kings 8:27).

Also, God said to the righteous Job, "Do you know the changes of heaven, or the events which take place together under heaven?" (Job 38:33).

The Lord Christ, Himself, confirmed the reality of heaven when He said to Nicodemus, "No one has ascended to heaven but He who came down from heaven, that is, the Son of Man who is in heaven" (John 3:13). Also in His words to Nathaniel who was surprised when he revealed to him one of the mysteries of his life, "And He said to him, 'Most assuredly, I say to you, hereafter you shall see heaven open, and the angels of God ascending and descending upon the Son of Man'" (John 1:51).

In His teaching of the Sermon on the Mount, He said "Do not swear at all: neither by heaven, for it is God's throne; nor by the earth, for it is His footstool" (Matthew 5:34–35); and "For assuredly, I say to you, till heaven and earth pass away, one jot or one tittle will by no means pass from the law till all is fulfilled" (Matthew 5:18). When the apostles were surprised at the submission of the demons to them in the name of Christ, He warned them and taught them, saying, "Nevertheless do not rejoice in this, that the spirits are subject to you, but rather rejoice because your names are written in heaven" (Luke 10:20). The Lord of Glory has spoken much about our portion and our inheritance in heaven.

Saint Paul the Apostle says, "See that you do not refuse Him who speaks. For if they did not escape who refused Him who spoke on earth, much more shall we not escape if we turn away from Him who speaks from heaven" (Hebrews 12:25).

There is an entire book in the Holy Bible, the Book of Revelation, that speaks of the heavens and all that is therein.

Moreover, God has revealed to some of the saints on earth a great extent of the majesty and glory of heaven:

Saint Stephen, the first martyr in Christendom, as he was being stoned by the Jews, "being full of the Holy Spirit, gazed into heaven and saw the glory of God, and Jesus standing at the right hand of God, and said, "Look! I see the heavens opened and the Son of Man standing at the right hand of God!" (Acts 7:55–56).

Saint Paul the Apostle saw visions that declared to him many things. In one of them, he was taken to the third heaven, which is Paradise. But he did not reveal anything that he saw. This could be because it is one of the mysteries that remains unrevealed to humans. He says that he "heard inexpressible words, which it is not lawful for a man to utter" (2 Corinthians 12:4). This could also be due to his own personal inability to describe it; "Eye has not seen, nor ear heard, nor have entered into the heart of man the things which God has prepared for those who love Him" (1 Corinthians 2:9). Nevertheless, Saint Paul has recorded for us the fact of heaven's existence.

As for Saint John the Apostle, a tremendous revelation has been declared to him, which he wrote down in the Holy Book known as the Book of Revelation—the last book in the New Testament. This book contains a symbolic description of heaven, and what will happen in the last days and the Day of Judgment. It also describes the joy of the saints in heaven.

Throughout the ages, visions and revelations have been declared to the martyrs, saints and confessors of the Lord Jesus, confirming the reality of the existence and glory of heaven. These visions and revelations motivated those martyrs in facing their ordeals and hardships, thus they stood firm to the end, until they received their unfading crowns.

An example of this may be found in the visions revealed to Perpetua, Troy's famous martyr, and her brother Saturus. The martyr Perpetua saw in a dream a large, golden ladder that reached from earth to heaven. The ladder was narrow and could only hold one person.

On both sides of the ladder were torture devices. At the bottom was a hideous dragon, standing on the first few steps, ready to attack those who try to climb the ladder. In the dream, Perpetua raised her head and saw her teacher and brother, Saturus, climbing the ladder. When he reached the top of the ladder, he told her, "Perpetua, I am waiting for you; but be careful that the dragon does not bite you."

Then, Perpetua answered, "In the name of the Lord Jesus Christ, he shall not hurt me." In boldness, she put her foot on the dragon, as if he were the first step of the ladder. Then she quickly began to climb. Finally, she reached the top of the ladder, where she saw a large garden, and in the midst of the garden a white-haired man dressed like a shepherd, surrounded by thousands dressed in white robes. There, Perpetua found the Good Shepherd, Jesus Christ, waiting for her, full of tender care for His sheep. The Lord then raised His head and said to her, "Welcome, My daughter." He called her and gave her a little cake, which she took from Him and ate. At this point, she heard the voices of those standing around, saying, "Amen." Perpetua then awoke from her sleep and tasted the sweetness in her mouth that she could not describe.

The night before her execution, Perpetua saw another dream. In her dream, the deacon Pomponius came to her jail cell, and knocked on the door violently. She went to open and saw him clothed in a richly ornamented white robe. He told her, "Perpetua, come, we are all waiting for you." She followed him until she came to an open arena. She knew it was there that the decisive fight would be.

She saw a horrible Egyptian man approaching from afar, with other men with him, also having the same desire to fight Perpetua. Then another man came and shouted in a very loud voice, "If this Egyptian is able to defeat her, let him kill her with his sword. But if she manages to kill him, let her come forward to take the palm branch."

He called for silence and then departed. They both drew closer to each other and began to fight each other. The Egyptian tried to grab her feet, but she hit his face with her heels. Then, she was lifted up in the air and began to beat him, took him by the head, and he fell on his face. She trampled him with her feet. Then, she went to the master of the ceremony. He gave her the palm branch, kissed her, and said, "Daughter, peace be with you." She then left through a large gate called the Gate of Life.

Saturus, Perpetua's brother and teacher (because he came before her in the Christian faith) narrates his dream. In his dream, he saw four angels that carried him and clothed him in a white garment. Then they brought him to his brothers, the martyrs, whom he knew on earth. He continues to say, "We saw a wonderful light, and heard voices saying unceasingly, 'Holy! Holy! Holy!'... When we were brought before the throne of the Lord Jesus, He gathered us in His embrace."

Contemporary People and Heaven

If we come to our present world, we find stories that have actually happened and are worth mentioning.

In this generation of ours, there lived one priest who

served and lived in one of the Menoufia villages. He was a saint who truly lived very simply. On the eve of Easter, when he was celebrating the Divine Liturgy, while he was saying, "He looked up towards heaven..." everyone noticed, especially the chanter, that the priest stopped his prayer.

When the chanter looked at him and found the priest gazing up, the deacon tried to draw his attention and completed the phrases of the prayer for the priest where he stopped, thinking that he might have forgotten the words. But this was in vain, for the priest kept silent. Another deacon tried to do the same, but again to no avail.

After the priest remained like this for almost ten minutes, he continued the liturgy from where he stopped. When the Divine Liturgy ended, and when the priest was taking off his vestments, one of the deacons asked him what had happened. But the father did not want to reveal what he had seen. The young deacon strongly insisted that the father explain what he had seen when he stopped praying.

After some great effort, the saintly father told him that as he was praying the words "He looked up towards heaven," he suddenly saw the dome of the church open, without any dome of the altar. He saw a bright ladder raised from the altar to heaven, and saw little angels ascending and descending on the ladder. He said he only stopped for a little while to enjoy this marvelous scene! This is what happened when God revealed the mysteries of heaven to one priest!

I shall share another true story. I knew a layman who

is now in heaven. He lived a very blessed life with God. I loved him dearly because of his righteousness. He too was reciprocal in his love and friendship. He was much older than I was. This righteous man told me of a vision he had seen himself.

One day as he was sitting on a chair, taking a short nap, he was taken to paradise by an angel who escorted him. He began to introduce him to brightly transfigured people in this place. The angel began to mention some of their names saying, "This is Father Abraham, this is Father Isaac, this is David." While he was in this revelation, someone came to wake him up, and thus the man was unable to continue the vision. He rose, but he had wished he could have had the opportunity to continue this beautiful experience.

Furthermore, I have come to know another righteous person, a saint in Saint Antony's Church in Shobra, Cairo, the deacon named Habib Farag. This man departed at the age of twenty-seven. Amazingly, he wrote down in his own handwriting in his personal diary which he kept in his pocket the day and hour in which he would depart to heaven! His story is a magnificent one that impresses upon us great spiritual comfort. This young man began his life away from God. He used to live with his family, near Saint Antony's Church. The servants there were driven to bring him and insisted that he attend the Bible study lessons in the church.

At first, he refused to go, but after their insistence, he accepted to go on one condition—that he would attend only one lesson. If he liked it, he would attend more of those meetings, but if he did not like it, he would not want to see the faces of those servants again. The young Habib attended the Bible Study and the grace of God touched his heart. The same night, the Holy Virgin Mary appeared to him in a dream. She took him by his hand to hell and said to him, "This is hell, and these are the wicked ones who await the Judgment." This scene moved him tremendously, such that he was seized with fear and begged the Mother of Light to quickly take him out because of this terrible sight.

The Virgin answered his plea and took him to Paradise. There, he saw brilliant shining people, each of whom was sitting on a bright, beautiful seat. He recognized many of those in Paradise. As he was walking around with the Virgin in Paradise, he found an empty chair and no one sitting on it. He asked the Virgin in amazement, "Whose empty chair is this and who will take his seat?"

The Virgin answered, "Do you not know whose chair this is? It is yours, if you follow Christ!" The dream ended with these exhilarating words. Habib woke up and lived a life of chastity, constant prayer and struggle to attain this empty seat that was awaiting him. This is the story of a young man who witnessed heaven while still in the flesh.

God's heavenly manifestations are still occurring to many people. The most beautiful of those heavenly manifestations may have been the one that happened on April 2, 1968, when the Virgin Mary, the Mother of Light, appeared on top of the church by her name in Zeitoun, a suburb in Cairo. This miraculous apparition was seen by thousands of people of different religions, ages, social levels and races. This apparition continued for several months. It was accompanied by many healing miracles and marvelous wonders to the sick, both Christian and non-Christian.

In addition to this, the apparition was the cause for the repentance of many. I, myself, saw the Virgin at the time of her apparition, but it was only for a few moments. There was one time, though, when the apparition remained for two and a half hours!

Now, after all of this evidence, can anyone deny the existence of heaven?! The mere objection does not deserve any kind of answer. It is like the blind who deny the existence of the sun, despite its reality, strength and beauty. Heaven is a confirmed fact—a fact that can never be doubted in the least bit. If we deny this truth, then we are denying our very own existence!

3

Holy, Holy, Holy: The Majesty of Heaven

We read a great deal about the lengthy and varied ways of torture that the confessors endured. The martyrs joyfully accepted death for the sake of obtaining heaven. We also know of the strife offered by the ascetics, worshippers and saints for the same purpose. These people, who endured to the end, were not foolish when they offered all of these sacrifices and sufferings. They surely did so for the sake of something far better. They were thoroughly assured of their purpose, which was heaven. But is heaven worth these tremendous sacrifices and this incredible self-denial?

What attracts the faithful towards heaven more than anything else is the fact that it is God's dwelling. The saints and the believers trust that they will be in heaven with God forever. Christ said, "In My Father's house are many mansions; if it were not so, I would have told you. I go to prepare a place for you. And if I go and prepare a place for you, I will come again and receive you to Myself; that where I am, there you may be also" (John 14:2–3). This means we shall be with Him in heaven!

What we know about heaven is very little compared to what we do not know. But our lack of knowledge about what is in heaven does not mean we are absolutely ignorant of everything about it. Even if our knowledge is very minimal, our knowledge about it is sufficient to enrich our faith and eagerness for our heavenly homeland.

It is in the Book of Revelation that we particularly know of God's words. This assuredly speaks of the matters to come and of eternal life. The book draws an entirely glorious and joyful picture of life to come. We tackle this subject of the glory of heaven in three points:

The Beauty of God's City

1. The City in General

God's city, heaven, and heavenly Jerusalem are all synonyms of the same thing. The witness, Saint John says, "Now I saw a new heaven and a new earth, for the first heaven and the first earth had passed away. Also there was no more sea" (Revelations 21:1). What is the meaning of the new heaven and the new earth? Saint John also says, "Then I saw a great white throne and Him who sat on it, from whose face the earth and the heaven fled away. And there was found no place for them" (Revelations 20:11). This means that the present earth and heaven, in their materialistic state, have disappeared, and instead came "a new heaven and a new earth." According to the words of Saint Peter, "We, according to His promise, look for new heavens and a new earth in which righteousness dwells" (2 Peter 3:13).

The first heaven was the place of the angels. Sometimes, Satan would enter it to be in God's presence to complain about some believers, as we read in the book of Job: "And it came to pass one day, that behold, the angels of God came to stand before the Lord, and the devil came with them. And the LORD said to the devil, "From where have you come?" And the devil answered the LORD and said, "I have come from compassing the earth, and walking up and down in the world." And the LORD said to him, "Have you diligently considered My servant Job, that there is none like him on all the earth, a blameless man, true, godly, abstaining from everything evil?" Then the devil answered, and said before the LORD, "Does Job worship the Lord for nothing? Have You not made a hedge about him, and about his household, and all his possessions round about? And have You not blessed the works of his hands, and multiplied his possessions upon the land? But put forth Your hand, and touch all that he has, and he will curse You to Your face!" (Job 1:6–11; 2:1–5).

Can you imagine Satan standing before the Lord and complaining about His believers?! But this is what Saint Paul the Apostle refers to when he says, "Who shall bring a charge against God's elect? It is God who justifies" (Romans 8:33). This was well justified in the book of Revelation by Saint John, "Then I heard a loud voice saying in heaven, "Now salvation, and strength, and the kingdom of our God, and the power of His Christ have come, for the accuser of our brethren, who accused them before our God day and night, has been cast down" (Revelations 12:10).

Even though the first heaven was the place of angels, yet Satan sometimes used to enter into God's presence to complain about some of the believers. Instead of this first heaven, there came a new one, full of the saints. Satan will not step inside of it, for he will be "cast into the lake of fire" (Revelations 20:10). The Lord Jesus also referred to the extinction of the present heaven and earth when He said, "Heaven and earth will pass away, but My words will by no means pass away" (Matthew 24:35). Moreover, in Hebrews, Saint Paul the Apostle referred to this: "You, LORD, in the beginning laid the foundation of the earth, and the heavens are the work of Your hands. They will perish, but You remain" (Hebrews 1:10–11).

This concerns the heaven and the earth, but what about the verse that says, "there was no more sea" (Revelations 21:1)? There is more than one reason for saying the sea will be no more—for the sea symbolizes separation. The seas in our world are known to separate and divide the world's continents, its regions and its peoples. The heavenly city is one perfect unit, without division or separation among its members. The sea also symbolizes the disturbance, uproar, worry and mystery. "But the unrighteous shall be tossed as troubled waves, and shall not be able to rest" (Isaiah 57:20). Eternity in heaven has no confusion, disorder or worry. Also, the salty waters of the sea refer to bitterness, which has no place in heaven.

2. Discovering God's City

If we want to describe God's city, we shall not find anything more descriptive than what Saint John mentioned in the Book of Revelation: "And he carried me away in the Spirit to a great and high mountain, and showed me the great city, the holy Jerusalem, descending out of heaven from God, having the glory of God. Her light was like a most precious stone, like a jasper stone, clear as crystal. Also she had a great and high wall with twelve gates, and twelve angels at the gates, and names written on them, which are the names of the twelve tribes of the children of Israel: three gates on the east, three gates on the north, three gates on the south, and three gates on the west. Now the wall of the city had twelve foundations, and on them were the names of the twelve apostles of the Lamb. And he who talked with me had a gold reed to measure the city, its gates, and its wall. The city is laid out as a square; its length is as great as its breadth. And he measured the city with the reed: twelve thousand furlongs. Its length, breadth, and height are equal. Then he measured its wall: one hundred and forty-four cubits, according to the measure of a man, that is, of an angel. The construction of its wall was of jasper; and the city was pure gold, like clear glass. The foundations of the wall of the city were adorned with all kinds of precious stones: the first foundation was jasper, the second sapphire, the third chalcedony, the fourth emerald, the fifth sardonyx, the sixth sardius, the seventh chrysolite, the eighth beryl, the ninth topaz, the tenth chrysoprase, the eleventh jacinth, and the twelfth amethyst. The twelve gates were twelve pearls: each individual gate was of one pearl. And the street of the city was pure gold, like transparent glass. But I saw no temple in it, for the Lord God Almighty and the Lamb are its temple. The city had no need of the sun or of the moon to shine in it, for the glory of God illuminated it. The Lamb is its light" (Revelations 21:10–23).

This is God's city . . . more glorious than any human language, so how can we possibly describe it?! We shall try to contemplate on what Saint John has recorded in this marvelous description of God's city, so we can deduce for ourselves spiritual consolation.

a. The entire city is made of pure gold.

Saint John says that the city was entirely made of pure gold. There is no doubt this description is symbolic. You can imagine how much people rush and fight in the whole world to possess gold. It is rare and very expensive. People may even reach the point of losing friendships and relationships for the sake of possession this precious metal! Imagine this brilliant gold in people's eyes here on earth being trodden upon by feet in heaven. This gold is trodden by the feet of the saints in the Heavenly Jerusalem. We have said that gold in heaven is only symbolic; it certainly refers to something that surpasses its earthly value.

If we meditate also as to what the pure gold refers to, we discover that it refers to the riches of the owner of this city as well as the riches of its inhabitants. This pure gold is similar to glass or pure crystal. What does this mean? This refers to purity of the life experienced by the inhabitants of this city. It is Christ who has proclaimed, "Blessed are the pure in heart, for they shall see God" (Matthew 5:8).

b. The city from the outside.

The city from the outside has God's glory. Its brilliance is like the most precious stone, which is jasper. The city from the outside is covered by God's glory, which is the reason why it has an amazing brilliance. At this point, we recall what happened to Moses the prophet when he went up to Mount Sinai to receive the commandments from God. Once he had come down from the mountain, his face shone so brightly that the people were afraid to come near him. Therefore, he put a veil over his face to cover his brilliance (Exodus 34:29–33).

Saint Paul commented on the story of Moses' shining face: "But if the ministry of death, written and engraved on stones, was glorious, so that the children of Israel could not look steadily at the face of Moses because of the glory of his countenance, which glory was passing away, how will the ministry of the Spirit not be more glorious?" (2 Corinthians 3:7–8). If this is what happened to Moses just from his encounter with God on the mountain, how much more can the city of God be like—the dwelling place of God Himself?!

c. The city was of equal measurement.

"The city is laid out as a square; its length is as great as its breadth" (Revelations 21:16). This refers to perfection. The city is perfect with regards to its length, width and height. Thus, those who dwell in it must be perfect.

d. The fence of the city.

The fence of the city surrounded its four sides. If we change those measurements mentioned in the book of Revelation to the measurements used today, then we shall find that the length of one side is equal to 1500 miles, or 2400 kilometers (12,000 cubits, where 1 cubit = 210 meters). The numbers are symbolic and refer to the immensity of the heavenly city. But why are there large and tall fences? God answers, saying "But there shall by no means enter it anything that defiles, or causes an abomination or a lie, but only those who are written in the Lamb's Book of Life" (Revelations 21:27). Therefore, the high fences prevent every abomination and refer to the city's stability.

Moreover, the walls were made of the fine stone, jasper, which is a metal solid rock that is of crystal green and varied colors. Its colors vary from reddish brown to pure, transparent crystal. Some believe it is a diamond. The solidity of the jasper refers to God's power that protects heavenly Jerusalem.

e. The goal of the city measurements.

The city has twelve doors, each in a different direction of which is an angel. On the doors are written the twelve names of the tribes of the children of Israel. The city wall has twelve foundations on which are written the names of the twelve apostles of the Lamb.

We notice at this point the repeated use of the number twelve and its multiples. The doors are twelve in number; there are twelve angels; the names of the tribes of the Israel are twelve; the walls have twelve foundations on which are written the names of the Lamb's twelve apostles. We also notice the other numbers of the city measurements are the multiples of the number twelve. What does all of this mean? The number twelve points to the kingdom of God and to the sons of that kingdom. The number 1,000 refers to heaven. Thus the meaning of its measurements in full is 12,000 cubits. Thus, it is large enough for all of the sons of the kingdom.

f. The names written on it.

On the twelve doors are written the twelve names of the twelve tribes of Israel, whereas the names of the Lamb's twelve apostles are written on the city walls (Revelations 21:12, 14). This refers to the fact that this city has combined the tribes or the men of the Old Testament with the apostles of the Lord Jesus, that is, the men of the New Testament, because it is one Church that gathers the believers in Christ of both the Old and New Testaments.

As for the Jews who have deviated from the Church and who have refused to believe in Christ, by doing so, they no longer have a place in heavenly Jerusalem because the spiritual affiliation has been taken away from them. This is according to what the Lord Jesus, glory be to Him, said openly to the unbelieving Jews, "Therefore I say to you, the kingdom of God will be taken from you and given to a nation bearing the fruits of it" (Matthew 21:43). The Lord speaks again even more clearly, "And I say to you that many will come from east and west, and sit down with Abraham, Isaac, and Jacob in the kingdom of heaven. But the sons of the kingdom will be cast out into outer darkness. There will be weeping and gnashing of teeth" (Matthew 8:11–12).

g. The city doors.

The city has twelve doors; three on every side: the east, west, north, and south. These doors are never shut (Revelations 21:25). But why are there these three doors on every side? This could mean this city accepts dwellers with no partiality, from every corner of the earth.

Therefore, God's city is open to all believers, from all nations of the world. Let us contemplate on what Saint John says that each door is one of single pearl. Can you imagine there is a pearl so big that it could be a door?! The biggest pearl the world knows does not exceed more than 56 grams in weight. But in heaven, we find the entire door is one single pearl. I wonder how many tons can the weight of such a pearl be?! All of these are signs that point to the magnificence and brilliance of heaven, as well as the riches and glory of God in heaven. The pearl refers to the Lord Jesus, who is the invaluable and priceless pearl: "Again, the kingdom of heaven is like a merchant seeking beautiful pearls, who, when he had found one pearl of great price, went and sold all that he had and bought it" (Matthew 13:45–46).

Everyone who enters through the doors of this city should have sold the world with all its passions and temptations, and he should have purchased this expensive pearl, which is the Lord Jesus Christ. On the other hand, the Lord Jesus speaks of Himself as the door: "I am the door. If anyone enters by Me, he will be saved" (John 10:9). In this way, no one will be able to sneak in to the heavenly city in some way or another. If he wants to enter, he should go through the door, and the door is Jesus Christ.

Three doors facing the four directions are symbolic of the Holy Trinity, which is the only way to human salvation. The angels on each door refer to the impossibility of any forbidden one to sneak into this holy city.

h. The city's foundations.

The foundations of heavenly Jerusalem are adorned with precious stones: jasper, sapphire, chalcedony, emerald, sardonyx, sardius, chrysolite, beryl, topaz, chrysoprase, jacinth and amethyst. The gates have "names written on them, which are the names of the twelve tribes of the children of Israel" (Revelations 21:12). This is in accordance with what Saint Paul the Apostle said, "built on the foundation of the apostles and prophets, Jesus Christ Himself being the chief corner stone" (Ephesians 2:20).

The precious stones with which the city foundations have been built refer to the divine virtues granted by God in this life for our adornment. The foundation on which we build our eternity is the divine virtues that God grants us as a down payment in life through our strife. Thus, we see Christ comforting the striving Church through the prophet Isaiah, saying, "'Afflicted and outcast, you have not been comforted; behold, I will prepare carbuncle for your stones, and sapphire for your foundations;...There is an inheritance to those who serve the Lord, and you shall be righteous before Me,' says the Lord" (Isaiah 54:11, 17).

Does this not point to the virtues that adorn the believers in heaven? We notice, moreover, that these precious stones are of different colors. With a bit of contemplation, we notice that these colors are the basic ones from which light is composed, and Christ is the true Light! These colors also compose the rainbow of light that appeared after the flood that is a landmark of the covenant between God and mankind—that He would not destroy the world again.

Furthermore, we notice the blue and green prevail among the colors of the precious stones. What is amazing is that scientists say that these colors are the two most relieving ones to look at and experience. There is no doubt that this will happen to the redeemed ones in God's city. In addition to those two colors, there is red, which refers to the blood by which we have been redeemed!

Life in the City of God

1. How Shall We Live in Heaven?

This is a question often asked, but we are completely unable to fully grasp the essence of heaven. Unfortunately, our knowledge and information of heaven are still very limited. This could be because there is nothing like it in our material world. So, we must draw the analogy between our world and heaven. At the same time, heaven is greater and more magnificent than any language can express. As Saint John said in his vision, "Now I saw a new heaven and a new earth, for the first heaven and the first earth had passed away" (Revelations 21:1).

It is so hard to imagine the happiness in heaven and all that is therein, with an earthly concept and the world's materialistic standards. We are facing a very new and serious situation. Thus we understand the words of the Lord Jesus that introduced His parables about the kingdom, "The kingdom of heaven is like..." This is only an analogy. Christ, glory be to Him, was attempting to draw the heavenly concept a bit closer to the people. All that was said about heaven was only an image or "shadow" as mentioned by Saint Paul the Apostle, "For the law, having a shadow of the good things to come, and not the very image of the things" (Hebrews 10:1).

Isaiah the prophet also well said, "O that You would tear the heavens open and would come down! From of old we have not heard, neither have our eyes seen a God besides You, and Your works which You will perform to them that wait for mercy" (Isaiah 64:1,4 NJB). The words, "O that You would rend the heavens open and come down" refer to the Incarnation. There is no one who is able to tell us what is in heaven except He who tears the heavens and comes down, that is Jesus Christ. This is exactly what Jesus said in His words to Nicodemus about one of the mysteries of Christianity which is the second birth, "If I have told you earthly things and you do not believe, how will you believe if I tell you heavenly things? No one has ascended to heaven but He who came down from heaven, that is, the Son of Man who is in heaven" (John 3:12–13).

Saint John the Evangelist confirms the same meaning in his words, "No one has seen God at any time. The only begotten Son, who is in the bosom of the Father, He has declared Him" (John 1:18).

Saint Paul the Apostle, when given the opportunity to go to the third heaven, was unable to give us an accurate and detailed description of what he saw there. Rather, he found it enough to confirm what was mentioned in the olden times by Isaiah the prophet, saying, "As it is written, 'Eye has not seen, nor ear heard, nor have entered into the heart of man the things which God has prepared for those who love Him" (1 Corinthians 2:9).

In this very way we can see that due to man's inability to describe the heavens positively, Saint Paul has described it negatively. Instead of saying it is this or that, he resorts to the negative attitude, and says, "eye has not seen." Thus, man confirms the fact of his inability and his weakness in describing heaven. When Saint Paul tells the story of being taken to heaven, he says, "I know a man in Christ who...was caught up into Paradise and heard inexpressible words, which it is not lawful for a man to utter" (2 Corinthians 12:2, 4).

In this way, Saint Paul took us to an immense maze, in which we could only discover that heaven is extremely wonderful and that the heavenly glory is far greater than any description possible, which cannot be absorbed by our own minds. And this is the truth, for the heavens and the heavenly kingdom are a sealed mystery. Its seal can never be unlocked, nor can we be happy with it in any earthly bliss or worldly experience.

2. What is Heaven?

To answer this question, we can only hold on to the few words supplied to us by divine inspiration about heaven.

a. There is no hunger or thirst; no heat or cold in heaven.

Even Christ, glory be to Him, has blessed in His famous Sermon on the Mount "those who hunger and thirst for righteousness sake." Saint John describes the righteous in heaven and says, "They shall neither hunger anymore nor thirst anymore; the sun shall not strike them, nor any heat" (Revelations 7:16).

Why will they not hunger or thirst? What will they eat and drink? God says in the Book of revelation, "To him who overcomes I will give to eat from the tree of life, which is in the midst of the Paradise of God...[and] I will give some of the hidden manna to eat" (Revelations 2:7, 17). As for their drink, He says, "the Lamb who is in the midst of the throne will shepherd them and lead them to living fountains of waters" (Revelations 7:17).

b. There is no crying or sighing; no suffering or sickness.

Saint Augustine says, "the holy days following the Lord's resurrection (the Holy Fifty Days) mean our life after the resurrection. This is in accordance with the forty days prior to the Resurrection (the Great Lent), which means the life of struggle in the test of death. Likewise, the days following Lent mean our other life to inherit and reign with the Lord. Our present life is like the forty days prior to Lent."

In this way our Holy Church, guided by the Holy Spirit makes clear to us the highly spiritual mysteries in the rituals, and what is made tangible through inner feelings. There is no abstinence or prostrations for fifty days after the Resurrection because it is a model of our life in heaven when we will reign with the Lord, where there will be no hunger or thirst! It is noteworthy to mention that our Church, on the Night of the Apocalypse (Bright Saturday), the entire book of Revelation is read very accurately because we are beginning the Holy Fifty days, which are similar to being in heaven. In these days, the Church forbids any fasting and all signs of humiliation, such as the prostrations or metanoias. As it is written in the Book of Revelation, "the Lamb who is in the midst of the throne will shepherd them ... and God will wipe away every tear from their eyes ... for the former things have passed away" (Revelations 7:17, 21:4).

"The former things have passed away!" This is an understood fact; for sorrow, pain and weeping are all the result of sin. The Scholar Tertullian comments on this by saying, "God wipes away every tear previously wept, for it could not be dried up unless wiped away by divine mercy."

c. There are no passions or divisions in heaven.

Surely there are no passions or divisions. Rather, there is absolute concord in the spiritual and glorified body. "The body is sown in corruption, it is raised in incorruption. It is sown in dishonor, it is raised in glory. It is sown in weakness, it is raised in power. It is sown a natural body, it is raised a spiritual body. There is a natural body, and there is a spiritual body" (1 Corinthians 15:42–44).

For instance, in heaven there is no sexual passion that leads man to any kind of deviation or inward conflict. This is clear when the Lord Jesus, glory be to Him, answered the Sadduceesregarding the woman who was married to a husband who died and bore him no children. She then married his six brothers, one after the other, so as to raise up lineage for their brother. After everyone died, the woman died as well. They asked Him, "In the resurrection, whose wife of the seven will she be? For they all had her." The Lord's answer clearly shows their materialistic thinking: "You are mistaken, not knowing the Scriptures nor the power of God. For in the resurrection they neither marry nor are given in marriage, but are like angels of God in heaven" (Matthew 22:27–30).

Moreover, there is no place for the tempter in heaven. There is no place for Satan. In the olden times, Satan was able to reach the Garden of Eden and overcame Adam and Eve by making them both fall. But he will not be able to set foot in God's heavenly city.

d. There is no jealousy, envy or disagreement in heaven.

In heaven, there is also no jealousy, envy or disagreement. Rather, there is absolute accord and perfect love among all the saints there. The Psalmist foresaw all of this in a prophetic spirit and so he said, "See now! What is so good, or what so pleasant, as for brethren to dwell together? It is as ointment on the head, that ran down to the beard, upon the beard of Aaron; that ran down to the fringe of his clothing. As the dew of Hermon that comes down on the mountains of Zion; for there, the Lord has commanded the blessing, even life for ever" (Psalms 132:1–3). This prophesy is about heaven; as evident in his saying, "there, the LORD has commanded the blessing, even life for ever." Heaven is where love prevails among its inhabitants.

e. There is no cursing in heaven.

The curse was the result of sin. After the first man had committed sin, God told him, "Cursed is the ground in your labors" (Genesis 3:17). In this way the earth was cursed because of Adam. Then God cursed man through Cain after he had killed Abel, his brother, "And now you are cursed from the earth" (Genesis 4:11). But in the new ground, which is heaven, Saint John says, "And there shall be no more curse" (Revelations 22:3).

f. There is no darkness in heaven.

Darkness and night do not exist in heaven. "There shall be no night there: They need no lamp nor light of the sun, for the Lord God gives them light. And they shall reign forever and ever" (Revelations 22:5). God Himself is the Light...He is the eternal light, after "the sun will be darkened, and the moon will not give its light; the stars will fall from heaven, and the powers of the heavens will be shaken" (Matthew 24:29). The light in God's city will not be physical light, but God will be the Light of heaven. In this way, we understand the prophet's words of old, "In Your light we shall see light" (Psalms 35:9).

g. There is no ignorance in heaven, only perfect knowledge.

We have been living in the body by faith in the world.

Faith offers us knowledge, as in a mirror, similar to a puzzle. But in heaven, we shall live a life of visualization. We shall see everything face to face. As Saint Paul says, "For we know in part and we prophesy in part. But when that which is perfect has come, then that which is in part will be done away. When I was a child, I spoke as a child, I understood as a child, I thought as a child; but when I became a man, I put away childish things. For now we see in a mirror, dimly, but then face to face. Now I know in part, but then I shall know just as I also am known" (1 Corinthians 13:9–12).

I wish to add one more thing. When man was on earth, the created things gave him the desire and means to know God. Thus, Saint Paul says, "For since the creation of the world His invisible attributes are clearly seen, being understood by the things that are made, even His eternal power and Godhead, so that they are without excuse" (Romans 1:20). We know God through the visible creation. In other words, we come to know God through what we see in creation.

But the situation is reversed in heaven, for God will become the means by which we will know everything. It will be through Him that we know everything. He will be like a big telescope through which we can see, and in Whom we can see all the minute details.

h. We shall see all those who have attained the glory, and who have departed before us.

Is this all there is in heaven? Surely there is a lot. For

example, we shall see all those who have gone ahead of us to glory, everyone from Adam to the end of ages. We shall see all those whom we read about, those who have encouraged us through their autobiographies and biographies. We shall also see all of those who we asked to intercede or pray for us—whether they are angels, patriarchs, prophets, apostles, martyrs, confessors or hermits. We shall see all of those who have pictures and icons in the church.

Above all, we shall see our mother, the Holy Virgin Saint Mary. We have seen thousands of people crowding around the Church in Zeitoun to receive a blessing and witness her apparitions above the church. Many of them waited for hours. But in heaven, we shall see the Virgin and be with her. We shall see all of these saints face to face!

i. We shall hear the praises of the angels in heaven.

What else is there about heaven? There, we shall hear the praises of the angels, and shall even join them in their praises. When we hear a beautiful voice, we say this is an angelic voice. So how much more will our joy be when we shall be with the angels themselves, hearing them and chanting with them?! Contemplate on the beauty of what we shall see and hear that we may attain the blessing. The Psalmist said about this, "Blessed are those who dwell in Your house; they will praise You evermore" (Psalms 83:4).

Conclusion

The conclusion, dear brethren, is that in heaven we shall reign with God. Can you imagine this? Has not the Lord of Glory said, "Come, you blessed of My Father, inherit the kingdom prepared for you from the foundation of the world" (Matthew 25:34)? The weak and worthless man will reign with God! We certainly do not know our own worth in God's eyes. Although we are made of worthless dust, we have this worth by Christ's blood that has been shed on the Cross. In light of this, we are able to understand the words of Saint Paul the Apostle, "justified freely by His grace" (Romans 3:24). Yes, freely, for we have not paid anything and we were incapable of paying anything. Meditate on David's words: "who lifts up the poor from the earth, and raises up the needy from the dunghill" (Psalms 112:7).

God has revealed the depth of His love for mankind by lifting them up out of the dust so they will not only sit with princes, angels or saints, but He will allow them to sit with Him personally!

The Lord says in the Book of Revelation: "To him who overcomes I will grant to sit with Me on My throne, as I also overcame and sat down with My Father on His throne" (3:21). Has not the Lord of Glory Himself said, "In My Father's house are many mansions; if it were not so, I would have told you. I go to prepare a place for you. And if I go and prepare a place for you, I will come again and receive you to Myself; that where I am, there you may be also" (John 14:2–3)?

The conclusion is that we shall reign with God in the city of life forever—in this awesome city not built with human hands, but rather, "whose builder and maker is God" (Hebrews 11:10). It is the city whose inhabitants are only included in the Book of Life. It is the city that knows no death, sin, grief, birth or burial. The angels are its guards, and all of its inhabitants are saints!

The Peak of Joy and the Blessed Testimony

We will be blessed joyfully with the splendor of heaven, because of its beauty and life; yet the greatest reason for the joy and spiritual awe in heaven is witnessing God, or as it is called, "the blessed witnessing and testimony." Our love for God when we are in the physical state is incomplete, and it will only be perfectly complete when we are in heaven.

Love is the fullness of joy. Love, in the human sense, always aims at possessing the beloved completely. This will also happen in heaven. There, the desire of the bride will be fulfilled as declared in the book of the Song of Solomon, "My Beloved is mine, and I am His: He feeds His flock among the lilies" (2:16).

No one will interrupt our harmony, and our peaceful joy. When the Lord Jesus was in the flesh, He hid His divine glory in His incarnation when He denied Himself and took the form of the servant, and came in the likeness of man (Philippians 2:7). But in heaven, we shall see Him as He is. Saint John the Beloved says the same of the Lord: "Beloved, now we are children of God; and it has not yet been revealed what we shall be, but we know that when He is revealed, we shall be like Him, for we shall see Him as He is" (1 John 3:2).

The great saint and philosopher, Saint Augustine, says, "We shall see God and this is a great thing. Anything else would be absolutely crude and worthless. We consider ourselves joyful here if we live in peace, even though it is difficult to attain it in this life. But if we compare this joy with the one awaiting us, the former is miserable and full of toil. For joy is in God's eternal house; in His house is an endless feast prepared for us. It will continue forever with the heavenly hosts in God's vision, and in immortal magnificence...there you will be truly happy. You will be in need of nothing, and you will ask for nothing. Your affluent riches will be God Himself."

This awesome description is conveyed to our hearts by Saint Augustine. Despite all of this, we believe Christ's glory, the King enthroned in glory and majesty in heaven, is immeasurably greater than our human eyes could bear. Saint Paul the Apostle says about this, "[God] alone has immortality, dwelling in unapproachable light, whom no man has seen or can see, to whom be honor and everlasting power. Amen" (1 Timothy 6:16).

But can we comprehend the joy of this vision? All of those to whom such visions appeared, were seized with fear, shaken and fell on their faces! Ezekiel the prophet, long ago, recorded for us his brief glimpse of the glory of God when he wrote, "As the appearance of the rainbow when it is in the cloud in days of rain, so was the form of brightness round about. This was the appearance of the likeness of the glory of the Lord. And I saw and fell upon my face, and heard the voice of One speaking" (Ezekial 1:28–2:1).

The Lord Jesus has manifested very little of His glory in the transfiguration. All what happened was that His appearance changed before His three disciples who were with Him. "His face shone like the sun, and His clothes became as white as the light. And behold, Moses and Elijah appeared to them, talking with Him. Then Peter answered and said to Jesus, 'Lord, it is good for us to be here.'"

While he was still speaking, behold, a bright cloud overshadowed them; and suddenly a voice came out of the cloud, saying, 'This is My beloved Son, in whom I am well pleased. Hear Him!' And when the disciples heard it, they fell on their faces and were greatly afraid" (Matthew 17:2–6)

On another occasion the Lord Jesus manifested Himself to His beloved disciple John in the Revelation recorded by this apostle. Saint John saw Him: "His head and hair were white like wool, as white as snow, and His eyes like a flame of fire; His feet were like fine brass, as if refined in a furnace, and His voice as the sound of many waters...and His countenance was like the sun shining in its strength" (Revelations 1:14–16). When Saint John saw Him in this appearance, he "fell at His feet as dead" (1:17). But, in spite of all of this, this is not the magnificence of God's glory!

But how will this witnessing be fulfilled? Is it by means of the eyes? The Fathers say this blessed witnessing of God is not fulfilled by means of the eyes. Rather, it is by knowing Him in a mentally superb way that surpasses nature, and is direct, without any intercession. For God is Spirit and He can not be seen with physical eyes. This mental knowledge is different than knowledge of God by faith. In heaven, God will bless man's mental knowledge in his new nature so that it will be able to partake in this blessed witnessing.

Saint Augustine said a beautiful statement, "Eternal life is witnessing." This is what Christ Himself has said, "And this is eternal life, that they may know You, the only true God, and Jesus Christ whom You have sent" (John 17:3). Therefore, eternal life is that they know, witness and realize what they have believed in, and obtained what they were unable to realize. At this point, the mind sees what the eye has not seen, what the ear has not heard and what has not been conceived by any man."

Therefore, witnessing is not that of the physical eyes, but rather that the mind witnesses through knowledge. Moreover, it is not the witnessing by means of faith. Someone may ask, saying, "Will man not get bored if he lives doing the same thing and in the same place, even if this place is heaven?" Actually, no, for how can man get bored with all this glory and majesty around him?!

We have merely attempted to picture a little fragment of it. Despite this, let us recall Solomon's words, "All things are full of labor; a man will not be able to speak of them. Neither shall the eye be satisfied with seeing, neither shall the ear be filled with hearing" (Ecclesiastes 1:8). These are spiritual matters which the believer keenly desires to see while he is still in the body. Once he then sees them, how could he ever get bored?

Dear brethren, the greatest reward man is given in

heaven is that God will give Himself to man, as He said of old to our father Abraham. "Fear not, Abram, I am your shield. Your reward shall be very great" (Genesis 15:1). Just as God gives man Himself, likewise shall we too, be His forever. As David says in the Psalms, "I am Yours, save me" (118:94). In eternal life, we will be inseparable from God, for there is neither thing nor person that will be able to separate us from Him. There, the words of the bride are fulfilled, "My Beloved is mine, and I am His... [when] I found Him Whom my soul loves: I held Him, and did not let Him go" (Song 2:16, 3:4).

Dear brethren, this is the heaven we are awaiting. This is the heaven for which we are striving. This is the heaven for which we are enduring every hardship joyfully. We have calculated all of this, and it is enough!

4

Heaven's Creation

The Angels

Our understanding about heavenly creatures gives us several advantages:

First, it gives us a great link to the heavenly life while we are still living on this earthly and alien soil.

Second, we may understand more about the group of wicked angels—the devils —who are in constant war with us.

Finally, our eternal destiny is linked with them, since they will be our colleagues in heaven and in eternal life.

The subject is encompassed with mystery to a large extent! If we happen to know something, we discover that we are ignorant in many other things. Even the Holy Book, our basic reference, only provides us with very little information about angels, which is presented briefly and unintentionally. This may be so for a divine reason.

One thing we know—from our assumption or occasional imposition—is that our thick, material flesh that we are clothed in obstructs us from many things. The body depends on physical sensations, which do not realize or comprehend invisible spiritualities because they are more sublime than their nature. This is why when some angels appear to a group of humans, they actually come down to the level of our senses. They appear to us in a physical frame, even though they are actually more sublime than that.

1. The Meaning of the Words "Angel" and "Angels"

The word "angel"—as well as its plural form, "angels"— comes from the original Hebrew and Greek word, meaning a messenger sent to convey a message. It does not mean a particular frame or a sublime nature. In this concept, the name "angel" or "messenger" was attributed to some human categories.

It has been said of John the Baptist that he is an angel: "Behold, I send forth My messenger, and he shall survey the way before Me" (Malachi 3:1). The Lord Jesus Himself confirms this name when He said of John the Baptist, "See, I am sending My angel ahead of you, and will prepare Your way before You" (Matthew 11:10). For this reason, some artists in the old times drew John the Baptist as having two wings like the angels.

The bishops serving in the seven churches of Asia Minor have been mentioned as being angels in the book of Revelation, "I write to the angle of the church of..." (2:1,

8, 12, 18). "As for the mystery of the seen starts that you saw in my right hand, and the seven golden lampstands: the seven stars are the angels of the seven churches, and the seven lampstands are the seven churches" (1:20).

The second person of the Holy Trinity in the Old Testament was often referred to as "an Angel." The expression "God's angel" or "the Lord's angel" has been used in the Old Testament, particularly in the first books, so as to express the manifestation of God Himself. The proofs are many on this point. Compare, for example, Genesis 22:11, 16:7, 16:10, 16:11, 31:11, and 31:13.

We also read in the Old Testament about God's appearance in the image of man. An example of this is the three men who appeared to Abraham in Mamre (Genesis 18:2, 22). Also, the man who wrestled with Jacob, the father of fathers, all night long. The Holy Book says that after this wrestling, "And Jacob called the name of that place Peniel; for, he said, 'I have seen God face to face, and my life was preserved'" (Genesis 32:24, 30). Due to these explicit statements, there is no doubt these were divine manifestations, and that they were a symbol for the Incarnation of the Son that has been fulfilled in the fullness of time.

In the same way, Malachi the prophet spoke of the second person as "the angel of the covenant." After he had prophesied of John the Baptist as being the angel, or messenger, preparing the way before Him, he says, "Behold, I send forth My messenger, and he shall survey the way before Me: and the Lord, whom you seek, shall suddenly come into His temple, even the angel of the covenant, whom you take pleasure in: behold, He is coming, says the Lord Almighty" (3:1). Since the angel is a messenger, this name was attributed to the Lord Jesus because He was sent, "Just as the Father has sent Me, I also send You" (John 20:21). But the more specific meaning that is well known to us for the word "angel" and "angels" is the concept that we all know of, and this is the topic of our discussion.

2. Do Angels Really Exist?

There are some who deny the presence and existence of angels and devils. This is a corrupt idea that has its roots in the Old Testament. The Sadducees—who composed a big part of society at the time of the Lord Jesus and among whom were the priests and the chief priests—denied the existence of angels, the spirits and eternal life. Then what evidence is there to prove the existence of angels?

We shall answer this in mental evidence then in a documentary one:

a. The Mental Evidence. The universe in which we live is distinguished by the phenomena of progression. In it we find the earthly, the vegetation, the variable levels of living creatures, beginning with the earthly animals until man, who is the most civilized of the living creatures on earth. If this is the case, then it is logical that man cannot be at the last level of progression in the universe. Rather, it is possible and likely, that there are creatures above the level of man—the angels.

b. The Documentary Evidence. There are endless evidences

in the Old and New Testaments that prove the existence of angels. We shall try to be brief in mentioning models of these evidences:

(1) Old Testament Evidence:

We read in the book of Genesis that after Adam and Eve's fall, God appointed the Cherubim of the angelic ranks to guard the Tree of Life, "And He cast out Adam and caused him to dwell outside of the garden of Eden, and stationed the cherubim and the fiery sword that turns about to keep the way of the tree of life" (Genesis 3:24).

The manifestation of an angel to Hagar on the right of a spring of water in the wilderness, "on the way to Shur" (Genesis 16:7–11). The angel foretold her of Ishmael's children. He commanded her to return to her mistress Sarai, and to yield to her.

The two angels who came to Sodom and met Lot (Genesis 19:1–22).

The angel who stretched his hand on Jerusalem to destroy it and its people, "And the angel of the Lord stretched out His hand against Jerusalem to destroy it, and the Lord relented of the evil, and said to the angel that destroyed the people, 'It is enough now, withhold your hand' And the angel of the Lord was by the threshing floor of Araunah the Jebusite" (2 Samuel 24:16). David saw this angel.

The angel who appeared to Elijah the prophet when

he was asleep in the wilderness under the broom tree. He touched him and talked to him. He also offered Elijah a cake and a jar of water. He ate, drank and walked in strength due to this meal forty days and forty nights, until he reached God's mountain in Horeb (1 Kings 19:5).

(2) New Testament Evidence:

The appearance of the angel to Zachariah in Jerusalem in the temple, on the right hand of the incense altar. The angel heralded the birth of St. John the Baptist (Luke 1:11).

Archangel Gabriel appeared to the Virgin Mary and proclaimed the good news of the divine conception and the Savior's birth.

The appearance of the angel to St. Joseph the carpenter, more than once, when the Virgin Mary was betrothed to him (Matthew 1:20; 2:13, 19).

The angel who came down to move the water in the pool of Bethsaida. The first sick person to enter into the water after the angel's descent was healed of any disease he was suffering from (John 5:4).

The Lord Jesus spoke a great deal about the angels on more than one occasion. He said, "And I tell you, everyone who acknowledges Me before others, the Son of Man also will acknowledge him before the angels of God; but whoever denies Me before others will be denied before the angels of God" (Luke 12:8, 9).

The placement of angels is obvious in the New

Testament church. An angel appeared to Philip the preacher, one of the seven deacons, and urged him to stop on his journey from Jerusalem to Gaza, in order to meet the Ethiopian eunuch, the minister of Kendakah. Philip preached to him about the Lord Jesus Christ (Acts 8:26).

An angel appeared to Cornelius and said to him, "Your prayers and your alms have ascended as a memorial before God" (Acts 10:3).

There was also the angel who bought out all the apostles from jail (Acts 5:19).

The angel who delivered St. Peter from jail after Herod had decided to kill him so as to please the Jews (Acts 12:7).

The angel who appeared to St. Paul in a vision at night when he was traveling in a ship on his trip to Rome. The angel told St. Paul of his rescue, he and all those with him on the ship. Then St. Paul told those with him on the ship, "For last night there stood by me an angel of the Lord to whom I belong and whom I worship" (Acts 27:22).

When were the Angels Created? The scholars of the Holy Book agree that the angels were created on the first day when light was created, "And God said, 'Let there be light' and there was light" (Genesis 1:3). They based their opinion on the fact that angels are of a brilliant nature. At the same time there is no objection they could have been created before the world's formation. We assume this based on God's words to Job, "Gird your loins like a man, and I will ask you, and you shall answer Me!, 'Where were you when I founded the earth? Tell me now, if you have knowledge. Who sets the measures of it, if you know? Or who stretched a line upon it? On what are its rings fastened? And who is He that laid the cornerstone upon it? When the stars were made, all My angels praised Me with a loud voice" (Job 38:3–7). The "morning stars" here, refer to the angels or to a group of angels. Also the words "heavenly beings" have been mentioned more than once in the book of Job, and they refer to the angels. From these meanings, there lies the possibility that the angels have been created prior to the world's formation. This opinion is that of St. Gregory the Theologian.

3.The Nature of the Angels

Angels are spirits, without any doubt. This is confirmed by divine inspiration, as mentioned by the Psalmist, "Who makes His angels spirits, and His ministers a flaming fire," (104:4). However, in the previous verse, the word "messengers" is translated as "winds" since the Greek word *epnevma* ($\pi\nu\epsilon\upsilon\mu\alpha$) that has two meanings: "winds" and "messengers" or "spirits."

St. Paul the Apostle confirms the angels as being spirits: "of the angels He says, 'Who makes His angels spirits, and His ministers a flames of fire'" (Hebrews 1:7). He goes on to explain this meaning further saying, "Are they not all ministering spirits sent forth to minister for those who will inherit salvation?" (1:14).

Scholars have disputed among themselves concerning the nature of spiritual angels: whether they are spirits or if they have a spiritual form. As St. Paul the Apostle says, "there are also celestial bodies and terrestrial bodies... there is a natural body, and there is a spiritual body" (1 Corinthians 15:40, 44). Here, St. Paul attempts to clarify for us that after the resurrection we shall take spiritual, non-materialistic bodies—different than the bodies we now have on earth. Rather, we shall have spiritual bodies.

From this, came the question, "Are angels absolute spirits, or are they spiritual bodies?"

The opinion that supports the belief that angels are spiritual bodies is the opinion of the first church, since the time of the apostles. This belief was supported by St. Justin the Martyr, Athenagorus, Irenaeus, the scholar Tertullian of the second century; St. Clement of Alexandria of the third century; and St. Augustine of the fourth century. This remained to be the Christian church's opinion throughout the whole world (both east and west) until the year 1215. At that time, the fourth Lateran Council of the Catholic Church contradicted this creed, and taught that angels are merely spirits. However, according to the creed of the first church, angels are spiritual bodies, and not just spirits. We continue to keep this belief to this day.

Angels are of a sensible, alert and knowledgeable nature. This is an important point we shall speak more in detail about when discussing the fall of some angels. Angels actually have an awareness, knowledge and limited understanding. Even though this awareness, knowledge and understanding are limited, yet it exceeds those of man. Moreover, we are assured that the angels' awareness, their knowledge and their understanding are considered shorter and far less than the knowledge and understanding of God!

For man is a creature of limited mental abilities, and void of any knowledge. He is incapable of any awareness from the beginning and is contracted to his materialistic properties. The human mind is unable to estimate things properly unless after a lot of cross-examination. Man then keeps increasing in renewal until he comes to a stable fact concerning a certain subject. If the food for the human mind is science, then science, as we all know, is not firmly stabilized, but rather, develops constantly. Contrary to this is the angels' mind; for he realizes everything and is acquainted with the minutest details all at once, that is, not in steps and in gradation as with man. When I was a child, I did not realize what I now know. This means that my awareness developed continuously. This is not the case with the angels, for they realize everything and are aware of the detailed matters at once, without any gradation or steps, due to the mental light, which is one of the qualities pertaining to the angels.

This does not mean the knowledge of the angels is absolute; they do not know everything. We will tackle this when we speak of Satan, a fallen angel. Therefore, if angels do not know everything, thus the devils do not know everything either. It is of no avail that the naive ones go to sorcerers to come to know by means of the devils, hidden or future things. They are actually incapable of knowing everything. Therefore, the angels' knowledge is not absolute. It is rather limited, ineffective and contingent upon their jobs and missions in heaven. Even if they surpass man's knowledge, this is attributed to the spiritual nature of angels that enables them to reveal and know things humans can never discover or know due to their dense material bodies.

As for the angels, knowing God Himself and the Holy Trinity, as well as His divine mysteries, is surely knowledge that surpasses human knowledge—due to their being so close to God and due to their spiritual nature. St. Paul the Apostle says, "And without controversy great is the mystery of godliness: God was manifested in the flesh, Justified in the Spirit, Seen by angels" (1 Timothy 3:16). Therefore, the angels, by mental witnessing, realize some of God's mysteries, but not everything. Thus, we see St. Paul saying about this, "For what man knows the things of a man except the spirit of the man which is in him? Even so no one knows the things of God except the Spirit of God" (1 Corinthians 2:11). From this, we can conclude that the knowledge of angels surpasses that of mankind.

However, it is not absolute knowledge, but limited to what God reveals to them. For instance, it is God's will that they know about the divine conception. The Lord sends one of them to herald the good news to a virgin named Mary; thus they came to know of this subject. This also occurs during the Holy Family's Flight to Egypt. God sends one of His angels to St. Joseph the Carpenter, the betrothed to St. Mary, concerning this matter: "an angel of the Lord appeared to Joseph in a dream, saying, 'Arise, take the young Child and His mother, flee to Egypt, and stay there until I bring you word; for Herod will seek the young Child to destroy Him'" (Matthew 2:13).

The Lord Jesus referred to the fact that the angels are incapable of knowing absolute knowledge of all things. This was when He spoke of the end of the world and the last hour, "But of that day and hour no one knows, not even the angels in heaven, nor the Son, but only the

Father" (Mark. 13:32). St. Peter speaks of Christ the Lord's mission, His passion and His glories. He says that they are "things which angels desire to look into!" (1 Peter 1:12).

One of the most important qualities of angels is that their nature is immortal—that is, they do not die. To prove this, the Lord Jesus, to Him be the glory, has said, "but those who are counted worthy to attain that age, and the resurrection from the dead, neither marry nor are given in marriage; nor can they die anymore, for they are equal to the angels and are sons of God, being sons of the resurrection" (Luke 20:35–36).

4. The Numbers of Angels

They are so many that no one knows their number. In the fraction prayer of the Liturgy of St. Basil the Great, we pray, "He before whom stands thousands and thousands and endless numbers of holy angels and archangels: the cherubim, the seraphim and all the countless numbers of the heavenly hosts."

There are also many proofs in the Holy Book that prove the number of angels is immeasurable. Jacob, the father of fathers, saw great numbers of them and he said, "This is the camp of God" (Genesis 32:1, 2). Also, when king Araam was fighting Israel, Gehagi, Elisha the prophet's young man, saw big numbers of angels surrounding the mountain he was camping in (2 Kings 6:17). Moreover, Daniel the prophet, said that he saw, "a stream of fire rushed forth before Him. Thousands upon thousands ministered to Him, and ten thousand times ten thousand attended to Him" (Daniel 7:10).

The righteous Job said, "Is there any number to His armies?" (Job 25:3 NKJV). Furthermore, the Lord Jesus, to Him be the glory, when He was in the Garden of Gethsemane on the night of His passion, said to our teacher St. Peter, "Do you think that I cannot now pray to My Father, and He will provide Me with more than twelve legions of angels?" (Matthew 26:53). We do not even know how many those twelve legions of angels are! Also, St. Paul, in his epistle to the Hebrews says, "But you have come to Mount Zion and to the city of the living God, the heavenly Jerusalem, to an innumerable company of angels" (Hebrews 12:22). Finally, St. John describes to us in the Book of Revelation the tremendous numbers of angels he saw, saying "Then I looked, and I heard the voice of many angels around the throne, the living creatures, and the elders; and the number of them was ten thousand times ten thousand, and thousands of thousands, saying with a loud voice" (5:11).

It is clear, as a result of all this, that it is impossible to count the number of angels, in all their variable hosts, ranks, levels and kinds.

Satan and the Wicked Angels

The prevalent concept is that the devils were angels who have fallen. This concept is true, but when did this happen? How did it happen? And where? No one definitely knows. It seems that all the angels, after being created, went into some exam of which we do not know the place, the time or the manner. Due to this exam, the result was that they were divided into two groups: righteous angels and evil ones, who are the devils. The righteous ones have been called the holy angels, as the Lord Jesus, to Him be the glory, has said, "When the Son of Man comes in His glory, and all the holy angels with Him, then He will sit on the throne of His glory. All the nations will be gathered before Him" (Matthew 25:31).

They have also been called the chosen angels to confirm and to specify the fact that God has chosen them endlessly according to His wisdom, His justice and His foreknowledge. St. Paul the Apostle, our teacher, says, "I charge you before God and the Lord Jesus Christ and the elect angels that you observe these things without prejudice, doing nothing with partiality" (1 Timothy 5:21).

It is almost certain among the clerical scholars that the fall of the wicked angels or devils was the result of pride and arrogance. This assumption is based on what was mentioned in the book of Isaiah the prophet, "How has Lucifer, that rose of the morning, fallen from heaven! He that sent orders to all the nations is crushed to the earth. But you have said in your heart, 'I will go up to heaven, I will set my throne above the starts of heaven; I will sit on a lofty mount,on the lofty mountains toward the north; I will go up above the clouds; I will be like the Most High.' But now you shall go down to hell, even to the foundations of the earth!" (14:12–15). From this statement, it is clear that Satan tried to be like God. This means that the transgression of pride and arrogance was the cause of his downfall.

There is something else that should not be overlooked. Satan, in the first man's downfall, used the same temptation by which he had fallen. Satan called upon the first man to disobey and contradict God. This call was, at the same time, an invitation to godliness, "for God knew that in whatever day you should eat of it, your eyes would be opened, and you would be as gods, knowing good and evil" (Genesis 3:5). Just as Satan has fallen into the pit and into the abyss as an outcome of his sin of arrogance, likewise the first man faced his downfall!

It seems that Satan, called Sataniel, was an archangel, one of the cherubim. The rank of cherubim, as we pray in the Divine Liturgy, was a high position of the angels whose service was to the throne of God. Because Satan was an archangel, this means that due to his position, his service was directly linked to the divine throne without any intercession. Concerning this, Ezekiel the prophet says, "From the day that you were created you were with the cherub; I set you on the holy mount of God; you were in the midst of the stones of fire. You were faultless in your days, form the day that you were created, until iniquity was found in you. Of the abundance of your merchandise you have filled your storehouses with iniquity, and have sinned. Therefore you have been cast down wounded from the mount of God, and the cherub has brought you out of the mist of the stones of fire" (Ezekiel 28:14–16). In this way we know that Satan used to be a cherub, and he fell. But were there other angels who fell with him as well? And how can he fall while being an angel?

The angels, as we know, have a sensible, alert and

knowledgeable nature. He also enjoys a free will and correct mental evaluation. As a result of this, the angels do not misunderstand. If one of them tends to go the wrong way, this is not due to wrong evaluation or any kind of unawareness. Rather, it is due to insistence and voluntary action. In this, he is very different from man. The angel does not regret any wrongdoing he committed. He does not change because his tendency to wrongdoing is not the result of a lack of understanding. Rather, this is a firm will that does not change.

As for man, he often comes back to himself. After man commits sin, he regrets it when he realizes the sin in which he has fallen. He did not understand it when committing this transgression. As for the angel, his understanding is perfect and his vision is absolutely clear. Thus the fallen angels have no repentance or regret. If man fluctuates between good and evil, the angel in his full will tends to one of the two ways before going through it, not after he has started the course. Satan has therefore kept, after his downfall, all nature pertaining to that of an angel, be it in power, in ability or in understanding. Thus, all that is in the angels' nature is changed to evil and serving evil.

1. Satan's Names

The head of the evil angels who have fallen has various names, among which are:

"Satan"—a Hebrew word in its origin, meaning the "opposite" or "the resistant."

"The devil"—a Greek word in origin, meaning the

tempter or the one who complains, or the deceiver. The words Satan and the devil are the two most common names attributed to him

He was called by man other names in the Holy Book, including:

"Beelzebub" (originally Baalzabub)—the great god of the Palestinians (2 Kings 1:2).

"The adversary" or "the evil one"—In the Lord's Prayer, we pray "deliver us from the evil one" (Matthew 6:13). Also, "I do not pray that You should take them out of the world, but that You should keep them from the evil one" (John 17:15). Lastly, "But let your 'Yes' be 'Yes,' and your 'No', 'No.' For whatever is more than these is from the evil one" (Matthew 5:37).

St. Paul called him "Belial." "For what fellowship has righteousness with lawlessness? And what communion has light with darkness? And what accord has Christ with Belial?" (2 Corinthians 6:14–15).

"The ruler of the world." The Lord of Glory, Jesus Christ, said, "Now is the judgment of this world; now the ruler of this world will be cast out" (John 12:31).

"The prince of the power of the air." St. Paul the Apostle said about him, "the prince of the power of the air, the spirit who now works in the sons of disobedience" (Ephesians 2:2).

"The god of this age." In this way also St. Paul the apostle called him, "Whose minds the god of this age has blinded, who do not believe, lest the light of the gospel of the glory of Christ, who is the image of God" (2 Corinthians 4:4).

"The great dragon." The book of Revelation calls him as such, "The great dragon was cast out, that serpent of old, called the Devil and Satan, who deceives the whole world; he was cast to the earth, and his angels were cast out with him" (12:9).

2. Satan's Destiny

As for his destiny and all those who follow him, it is the eternal hellfire. Concerning this the Lord of Glory says, "Depart from Me, you cursed, into the everlasting fire prepared for the devil and his angels" (Matthew 25:41). St. Jude the apostle also says, "And the angels who did not keep their proper domain, but left their own abode, He has reserved in everlasting chains under darkness for the judgement of the great day" (Jude 1:6).

3. The Number of the Devils

We cannot know the number of the devils, for their number is very great. In the miracle of casting out the devils from the lunatic in the Gadarenes village, the Lord Jesus asked the devil what name he had. The devil answered saying, "My name is Legion;, for we are many" (Mark 5:8). The word "legion" means a military troop. St. Paul, when speaking of the devils, tells us that these troops are great in numbers, almost innumerable. He says, "For we do not wrestle against flesh and blood, but against principalities, against powers, against the rulers of the darkness of this age, against spiritual hosts of wickedness in the heavenly places" (Ephesians 6:12).

4. The Devil's Kingdom

In chapter ten of the book of Daniel the prophet, he mentions that the devil has a kingdom with organized armies, just as modern military armies. After Daniel fasted for twenty-one days and humbled himself before God, God sent him a wonderful angel, probably the archangel Gabriel, at the beginning of his humiliation. He did not reach Daniel, except after three weeks. The reason for this delay is that the devil to whom was assigned the leadership of the Persian region, faced Gabriel and managed to obstruct him from reaching Daniel and informing him of God's message. Therefore, the Archangel Michael rose to his rescue. In the same chapter that speaks of 'the devil' as the ruler of the Persian Kingdom, he refers to the ruler of Greece, another of the devil rulers, assigned over the Greek places (Daniel 10).

4. Facts to Know About the Devil

Based on the names assigned to the devil as mentioned in the Holy Book, concerning his qualities, his deeds and his victims, the following facts are revealed to us:

  a. The devil's material power is tremendous. He

destroys the material things and possessions. He leaves some people with inflicting diseases, insanity and deformities. This is obvious from Job's story. Also, we can see this in the miracles the Lord Jesus performed, as in the healing of the insane one (Matthew 12:22–24), and the crippled woman (Luke 13:10–16), and the people He cast out the devils from. As a result of all this, it is clear that Satan has the power and the authority to perform, but within the limitations that God allows. We shall tackle this last point shortly.

b. Satan's psychological power, and his impact on people's minds and souls. Satan is behind every war, shame, scandal, deceit, betrayal, misery and hardship. There are situations and sins man would never have been debased enough to enter unless Satan was behind it or motivating it. Examples of this are the fall of David the prophet and king, the denial of St. Peter the Apostle, and the betrayal of Judas Iscariot! Who can believe that the great David would fall, and that he would fall in the atrocious sin of adultery as well as the horrific sin of homicide? Is this the same David that God testified of in a manner not spoken of any other person in the Holy Book, saying: "I have found David the son of Jesse, a man after My own heart, who will do all My will" (Acts 13:22)? Despite this, David falls into sin! Satan's fingerprints are obvious in the story of David's downfall.

Also, St. Peter the apostle, whose heart was filled with enthusiasm, said to the Lord, "Lord, I am ready to go with You, both to prison and to death!" (Luke 22:33). And this was actually what happened. Before this, the Lord Jesus said to St. Peter, "Simon, Simon! Indeed, Satan has asked for you, that he may sift you as wheat" (Luke 22–31). As for Judas Iscariot's betrayal to his Master, it is so obvious that St. John the Evangelist said, "Now after the piece of bread, Satan entered him" (John 13:27).

c. Satan's aim when fighting people is to make chaos prevail and division to fall amongst them. Satan actually kills people. He destroys homes and societies. He divides people and arouses them against one another. Even though Satan does this among people, yet he is not divided against himself. This is evident from the Lord Jesus' words, for when they accused Him of casting out demons by the power of Beelzebub the ruler of the devils, He said to them, "Every kingdom divided against itself is brought to desolation, and every city or house divided against itself will not stand. If Satan casts out Satan, he is divided against himself. How then will his kingdom stand?" (Matthew 12:25–26).

d. Satan is obstinate, persistent, relentless, skillful, and stubborn. He has no shame; he does not retreat. All of this is explicit in the Lord Jesus' tribulation in the wilderness. In addition to all of this, after Satan had attempted every possible temptation and cunningness with Christ, to Him be the glory, in the wilderness, in the temple, and on the mountain top, St. Luke says, "Now when the devil had ended every temptation, he departed from Him until an opportune time" (Luke 4:13). That is, he left Jesus for a while, without becoming ashamed or departing from Jesus for good!

e. One of the most obvious characteristics of Satan is his trickery and mysterious way. When fighting with the weapon of arrogance, he makes man fall, yet we see him hiding in a most malicious way. He convinces man that there is nothing called Satan. He puffs up people, so they become haughty. When man becomes haughty, we see Satan shrinking, hiding, disappearing, and convincing man that he is everything, and that there is nothing called Satan, and that people are the devils.

f. His amazing deception. One of Satan's most effective weapons is his deception. The following story portrays the extent Satan is able to deceive man. It was said that Satan came up to a man, and he made the man believe he was on the verge of death. When the man got scared of facing death, Satan smiled at him cunningly, and told the man he is able to deliver him from death, but only on one condition. In great eagerness, the man showed his willingness to comply with any condition, so he would be delivered from death. Therefore, Satan said to him that he loved the man, and thus he was giving the scared man the option of three choices. He was to choose one and carry it out, so he would save him from death. He must chose either to kill his servant, beat his wife or drink liquor until he gets drunk. The man thought within himself and said,

"How terrible it is to kill my honest servant. I also love my wife, how can I beat her? The only option left was that of the liquor which seemed to be the least worst of the three options. He therefore bought the liquor and drank until he got drunk. No sooner had the liquor reached his senses than he began to behave indecently. When his wife came in to advise him to cease this indecency, he flared up in anger and beat her intolerably. When the servant heard her screams he came in to save his mistress from his master's hand. The liquor made the man think this was unheard of that the servant intervenes between a man and his wife. He thought the servant had personal motives for this intervention, and it could be motives that touch honor! At the peak of his wrath, he caught a deadly weapon and killed the servant. In this way Satan deceived the man, and he carried out Satan's three requests without being aware of it!

This is the methodical plot Satan uses. He pretends to be compassionate for his victims until he makes them fall into sin. The same system was used by Satan towards the Lord Jesus Christ, to Him be the glory, in His tribulation in the wilderness. He came forward to the Lord, as if telling Him, "I pity You for You have been fasting for forty days, eating nothing at all. Have pity on Yourself. If You are truly the Son of God tell these stones to become bread!" This is one kind of Satan's tricks. But the Lord Jesus overcame Satan in the three tribulations. Therefore, we should not believe the deception and the misleadings of Satan. The Holy Book says about Satan that he is a liar and the father of liars. The most impressive evidence of Satan's dexterity in deception could be what St. Paul the apostle warned us of saying, "And no wonder! For

Satan himself transforms himself into an angel of light" (2 Corinthians 11:14).

This discussion needs us to meditate more when we face magicians and those exorcists of the spirits. Unfortunately, we find naive and lost people who believe in these matters, even though they are entirely of Satan, who deceives by changing his appearance as if he is an angel.

g. His alert and watchful attitude. He fights in wakefulness, just as in sleep—in dreams that are shocking and defiled! He never ceases or sleeps. It is mentioned about one of the hermits to whom God gave the gift of casting out demons, that the hermit asked the devils when casting out of a man who was possessed by evil spirits, "How do you come out? Is it by fasting?" They answered, "We never eat anything." He said to them, "Is it by keeping awake and not sleeping?" They answered, "We never sleep." The hermit asked them, "Is it by departing from the world, as the hermit monks do?" They answered, "Our dwelling place is in the wilderness and the deserted places." The hermit then asked, "Then how is it that you are cast out?" They answered, "There is nothing that crushes us except humility."

God and Satan

As we are mentioning Satan's overwhelming power, his characteristics and his methods, skillful and deceiving as they are, it is essential to make clear some points that integrate the essence of our faith:

Even though Satan possesses great and terrible power, yet he cannot draw close to anyone to tempt him unless God allows him to do so. Is the believer going to fear Satan's power, whereas the Lord Jesus has promised us that not one hair of our head will fall without our Father's permission? Satan is absolutely unable to make any person fall or to tempt him unless God allows. The temptation itself is contingent, or has a condition from God, within the capability of this person.

Thus St. Paul the apostle says, "No temptation has overtaken you except such as is common to man; but God is faithful, who will not allow you to be tempted beyond what you are able, but with the temptation will also make the way of escape, that you may be able to bear it" (1 Corinthians 10:13). Therefore, every temptation that man falls into is allowed by God's permission.

This truth is absolutely clear in Job's tribulation. In the first and second chapters of the book of Job, we read that God allowed Satan to tempt Job within certain limits. In the first chapter, we read that Satan appeared before God and began to incite God against Job, saying, "Does Job worship the Lord for nothing? Have you not made a hedge about him and about his household, and all his possessions round about?" (1:9–10). But God limited the power of Satan to tempt Job, "Behold, I give all that he has into your hand, but touch not himself" (1:12). This was the first tribulation in which Job lost his possessions and his children. Despite this, he kept thanking God, "The Lord has given, and the Lord has taken away. As it seemed good to the Lord, so has it come to pass; blessed be the name of the Lord" (1:21). But Satan did not rest in peace; he stood before God complaining of Job saying, "Skin for skin! All that a man has he will give as a ransom for his life" (2:4). This means that man escapes with his skin, even if he loses all that he has. In the second tribulation God allows Satan to tempt Job again with certain limits: "Behold, I give all that he has into your hand, but touch not himself."

This issue has also been touched in the miracle the Lord Jesus made when healing the demon-possessed man in the village of Gadarenes. The devils asked the Lord Jesus, to Him be the glory, to go into the herd of swine (Luke 8:31–33; Mark 5:12–13). When the Lord, therefore, allowed them this, they went out of the man to the herd, and thus the swine rushed to the sea cliff, fell and were drowned. This is obvious proof that the devils are unable to do anything except it be within God's permission and limits.

It is well understood that if Satan were roaming freely, doing all that he wants to do, then the world and the entire universe would have been destroyed. Thank God, he is not free to inflict catastrophe upon humans, to afflict them or to tempt them unless it is within what God allows for the good of man, spiritually speaking. If God knows that such a tribulation would distance you from Him, then He would never allow it to happen. If someone goes far away from God due to a certain ordeal or tribulation, then this is his own will because he did not struggle lawfully as he should to overcome the temptation.

Sometimes, God allows Satan to manifest his material

power which may seem tremendous indeed, so that God Himself may show His own power and be glorified all the more. If Satan is strong, then God is undoubtedly stronger. This is very obvious when we think of what happened at the hands of Moses the prophet in Egypt. The magicians and fortune tellers were able to do some amazing things, just as Moses did. But after a short time, in the third plague (of the gnats), the magicians found themselves absolutely incapable, and they declared their failure to do the same thing, "This is the finger of God" (Exodus 8:19). This same matter is repeated at all times. This happened with the apostles and the saints. Therefore, it is God's purpose to manifest Satan's weakness when compared to the almighty power.

To be saved and delivered from Satan's deeds and his uprisings could never happen unless we rely on and resort to God, taking refuge in Him who is far stronger than any other power. Christ, to Him be the glory, has come to the world, as St. John says, to destroy Satan's deeds (John 3:17–20). The conflict will keep going on fiercely until the dragon and his wicked angels fall and be thrown into the lake of fire. In every tribulation in which man faces Satan, man experiences God's care. In the bitter tribulation of Job, we can see God's care and His hand very clearly. We can also see this clearly when the Lord Jesus told St. Peter about the tribulation that would soon befall Him and His friends, the apostles. "Simon, Simon! Indeed, Satan has asked for you, that he may sift you as wheat. But I have prayed for you, that your faith should not fail" (Luke 22:31–32). Notice and meditate on how God is behind every tribulation; for He tells St. Peter "he has asked," for St. Peter's sake, so his faith may not fail. Therefore, the

Lord's hand is behind every tribulation that befalls man.

Let us know very well that whenever we are victorious in a conflict with Satan, we have to feel confident and believe that God's hand is the factor that supported us and not our own personal strength. In such a situation, I wish we reiterate what Jacob has said long ago when running away from the face of Esau his brother; also, after he had seen the vision of the ladder that reached up to heaven, linking it down to the earth, "The Lord is in this place, and I did not know it" (Genesis 28:16).

The Righteous Angels

1. The Characteristics of the Angels

There is no doubt that the angels are much more exalted than humans, whether in sublimity, greatness, strength, wisdom or sanctity. Let us speak about some of their characteristics:

Their strength: the foremost quality of angels is their strength. This is why we find David the prophet saying, "Bless the Lord, all you His angels, mighty in strength, who do His bidding" (Psalms 103:20). St. Paul the apostle also refers to this saying, "when the Lord Jesus is revealed from heaven with His mighty angels in flaming fire" (2 Thessalonians 1:7–8). There is no better proof for this power than that of one single angel who killed in one night 185,000 soldiers of the army of Senaharib, king of Ashor (Isaiah 37:36). Another angel killed in one night all the Egyptian firstborn. Moreover in David the prophet's time, a third angel stretched out his hand so as to ruin the entire city of Jerusalem, if it were not for the mercy of God (2 Samuel 24:15).

Their holiness. This is a well-understood matter, for they are always there, in God's presence.

This is why they are called saintly angels.

Their wisdom. They are definitely greater in wisdom than humans, due to their nature, their life and their job. It cannot be reasonable the God commissions them to perform the most accurate of jobs without them having the excessive wisdom and understanding.

Their ability to move and be transferred. They do not need a long period of time to move from one place to the other, for they do not have material bodies that hinder their movement. In just one moment they can travel thousands of miles. Moreover, they can get rid of their material bodies due to their spiritual nature that allows them to penetrate through material.

2. Their Jobs

The jobs of angels are numerous and vary according to the rank of the angels themselves. There are angels who stand before God's throne; their job is to offer worship, kneel down, and praise God continuously. There are other angels who work as a link of communication between heaven and earth, or between God and people. A third team of angels has the job of serving mankind. We can divide the work of an angel into two parts: what concerns God and what concerns people. We can abbreviate this in the following:

a. Firstly: What concerns God. This includes deeds, among which the most important is ...

(1) Worshipping. This comes in the foremost place in the angels' jobs which concern God. God's worship comprises praise-giving and adoration. A vision has been revealed to Isaiah the prophet in which he saw the seraphim chanting and saying in constant praise, "Holy, holy, holy is the Lord of hosts; the whole earth is full of His glory" (6:3). At the time of the Savior's birth, St. Luke conveys to us a magnificent picture, "And suddenly there was with the angel (who brought the shepherds the good news of Christ's birth) a multitude of the heavenly host praising God and saying: 'Glory to God in the highest, and on earth peace, goodwill toward men!'" (2:13–14). Thus David cried out and said, "Praise Him, all His angels; praise Him all His hosts" (Psalms 148:2). This concerns the praise giving.

As for worship, St. John records to us what he saw in his revelation, "All the angels stood around the throne and the elders and the four living creatures, and fell on their faces before the throne and worshipped God, saying: 'Amen! Blessing and glory and wisdom, Thanksgiving and honor and power and might, Be to our God forever and ever. Amen'" (Revelations 7:11–12).

(2) The carrying out of God's judgment. An example of this is what is mentioned in the book of Acts of the Apostles about Herod, the king, who put on the royal garment, and got puffed up, to the extent that when he spoke the people said that was the "voice of a god and not of a man" (12:22). At this point, God sent an angel who struck him on the spot, because he "did not give the glory to God;" then the worms began to eat him up till he died (12:23). Moreover, St. John in his revelation records to us, "Then I heard a loud voice from the temple saying to the seven angels, 'Go and pour out the bowls of the wrath of God on the earth'" (Revelations 16:1). Therefore, the angels always carry out God's commands.

(3) The revelation of God's messages to mankind. These messages are variable ones. Either they are messages of encouragement and strengthening to perform a duty, as happened with Gideon (Judges 6:11–16); or messages of rebuke to a person, or to an entire nation. We also read about the messages of rebuke that God's angel carried to the Israelites (Judges 2:1–5). The angel could also be sent to convey a joyful message as happened with the birth of St. John the Baptist. This also happened with Archangel Gabriel's joyful good news to the Mother of Light, St. Mary, telling her of the birth of Jesus our Lord, the Savior of the world.

(4) In the last judgment. The Lord Jesus presents to us this lesson in the parable of the weeds and the wheat, in which He says, "The harvest is the end of the age, and the reapers are the angels ... so it will be at the end of this

115

age. The Son of Man will send out His angels, and they will gather out of His kingdom all things that offend, and those who practice lawlessness, and will cast them into the furnace of fire" (Matthew 13:39–42).

b. Secondly, what concerns the people

We have to know that the angels, who to fulfill God's purposes toward mankind, sometimes go into wars against Satan and his hosts. This is clear from what is mentioned in the book of Daniel (10) as we have previously said. Also, what is mentioned in the book of Revelation, where he says, "And war broke out in heaven: Michael and his angels fought with the dragon; and the dragon and his angels fought" (12:7). We summarize what the angels perform as services towards people in the following:

(1) The care towards the believers and guarding them. At this point we recall the words of the Psalmist David, "the angel of the Lord will encamp around those that fear Him, and will deliver them" (33:7). Also, the words of the chanter in the memorable Psalms, "For He shall give His angels charge over you, to keep you in all your ways. They shall bear you up on their hands, lest at any time you dash your foot against a stone" (90:11). Therefore, the angels take care of us, we the believers, and the protect us.

(2) Delivering the believers from all ordeals. The Holy Book is full of various examples where the angels

intervene, and they deliver many humans; among these is Jacob from the face of Esau his brother in Mehnaim (Genesis 32:1, 2). Also, the angels delivered God's people when departing from Egypt, until they settled in the land of Canaan (Exodus 14:19; 23:20). The angels, moreover, were the ones who protected and guarded Elisha the prophet, and his disciple Gehesi from the army of king Aram (2 Kings 6:16–17). It was also God's army who shut up the mouths of the lions against Daniel in the den (Daniel 6:22). "My God has sent His angel, and stopped the lions' mouths, and they have not hurt me." In addition to all of this, it was the angel who rescued St. Peter from jail, an issue that St. Luke devoted a whole chapter to in Acts 12.

(3) Sharing in the service of salvation regarding the believers. This may be the motive that urged the angels at the Savior's birth to chant the memorable, joyful hymn, "Glory to God in the highest, and on earth peace, goodwill toward men!"(Luke 2:14). The Lord Jesus Himself, to Him be the glory, makes this clear when He said, "Likewise, I say to you, there is joy in the presence of the angels of God over one sinner who repents" (Luke 15:10).

(4) Encouraging the believers. The angel encouraged St. Paul the apostle in his ordeal in the ship at sea, on his way as a bondsman to Rome. St. Paul conveyed these feelings to all those with him on the ship, "For there stood by me this night an angel of the God to whom I serve, saying, 'Do not be afraid, Paul; you must be brought before

Caesar; and indeed God has granted you all those who sail with you'" (Acts 27:23–24).

(5) Saving the Believers. Concerning this, we say that the angels are able, because of their nature, to work and to move without receiving an order from God to do so, because this is their job. St. Paul says, "Are they not all ministering spirits sent forth to minister for those who will inherit salvation?" (Hebrews 1:14). The angels, therefore, are free creatures who have the capability and the means, and they are to act within their specific job. Similar to this is the police officer who stands in the street. If a citizen asks for his help, he would help him immediately and come forth to rescue him or be quick to catch a thief or killer without reporting to the head of the state or even his direct boss, because this is his job.

In contrast, if he does not answer a citizen's cry for help with the pretext that he did not receive an order from the head of the state or his direct boss, he would be considered in that case as not fulfilling his job rightfully. Concerning this we say: it is our right, therefore, to call upon the angels directly without this being a disregard to God. This means that he who cries out, "Help me, you angel of God," is not in sin. We are only answering the trivial thinking of some people who denounce those who ask for help from Archangel Michael, for example. They attribute this cry for help as that of an atheist, even thought the angels are the officers of the spiritual army that liberates the believers and rescues them. Therefore, there is no kind of embarrassment if I resort to the help of the heavenly officers to protect me from the evil forces.

This is why our Coptic Orthodox Church called for the intercession and the help of the angels or the archangels, which is a correct teaching to adopt. We are not sinning against God when we do so, because this is one of the jobs the angels are commissioned to perform.

(6) Raising the believers' prayers to God. It is the angels who are presenting our prayers before God's throne. This has been declared to us by St. John in the book of Revelation, "Another angel, having a golden censer, came and stood at the altar. He was given much incense, that he should offer it with the prayers of all the saints upon the golden altar which was before the throne" (8:3). The angels also come in the churches and attend prayer meetings. We know of this through what St. Paul the apostle said when asking the woman to cover her head in praying, "For this reason the woman ought to have a symbol of authority on her head, because of the angels" (1 Corinthians 11:10). This means that the angels attend the prayers with us.

(7) Intercession for the believers. The ladder that Jacob saw in his dream—upon which the angels were ascending and descending, linking the earth to heaven—refers in its totality to the work of the angels. They carry help from heaven to mankind, and ascend with their needs, in the form of prayers and pleadings, and present them to the One on the throne (Genesis 28:12). Once, the angel interceded in Jerusalem saying, "Then the Angel of the

Lord answered and said, 'O Lord Almighty, how long will You have no mercy on Jerusalem, and the cities of Judah, which You have disregarded these seventy years?' And the Lord Almighty answered the angel that spoke with me good words and comforting sayings. And the angel that spoke with me said to me, Cry out and say, Thus says the Lord Almighty; 'I have been jealous for Jerusalem and Zion with great jealousy. And I am very angry with the heathen that combine to attack her: for as I indeed was a little angry, but they combined to attack her for evil.' Therefore thus says the Lord: 'I will return to Jerusalem with compassion; and My house shall be rebuilt in her,' says the Lord Almighty, 'and a measuring line shall yet be stretched out over'" (Zechariah 1:12–16).

(8) Carrying the spirits of the righteous ones to paradise. This job is obvious in the story of the rich man and Lazarus. The words to show this were said by the Lord Jesus Himself, to Him be the glory, "The beggar died, and was carried by the angels to Abraham's bosom" (Luke 16:22).

Their Ranks

Actually this subject is enveloped with a great deal of mystery, and we cannot discuss it in accuracy or details. We are ignorant of so much concerning it, but we shall tackle it as much as the Holy Book provides us with, as well as the church tradition and the sayings of the saintly church fathers. There is no difference among all the heavenly hosts regarding their nature. The difference is in their positions and their ranking. It is said that the heavenly beings are divided into three categories or ranks:

The first category includes the seraphim, the cherubim and the thrones (or seats). The second category includes the dominions, the authorities, the powers and the hosts. The third category: this includes the rulers of the archangels and the angels.

Unfortunately, we are ignorant of so much about the various angelic categories. Therefore, we think it enough here to mention what we know about some of them.

a. The First Category of the Heavenly Hosts: the Seraphim, the Cherubim and the Thrones.

(1) The Seraphim. It refers to those brightly lit in fire. It is said that this indicates their burning love for God. This has only been mentioned in Isaiah 6:1–7. We have referred previously to their constant praise-giving: 'Holy, Holy, Holy, Lord of hosts; His glory fills the entire earth!' From this we can deduce and say that the seraphim ritual is the praise giving ritual, and the constant presence before God's throne and being blessed with the divine presence. The Holy Book has not mentioned for this category any kind of job in serving the people. The seraphim have six wings: two wings to cover their faces, two others to cover their feet, and two others to fly with. The covering of the face is symbolic of the reverence and honoring of God; the covering of the feet is symbolic of submission and the feeling of weakness and impurity before the holy God. As

for their cry, they continually say, "Holy, holy, holy is the Lord of hosts; the whole earth is full of His glory" (Isaiah 6:3). This refers to the absolute submission to God and the zeal for His glory. They are asking that God's glory may fill the entire earth.

(2) The Cherubim (singular cherub). It means "filling the world" or "full of knowledge." This host has often been mentioned in the Holy Book, and they are probably the first to be mentioned in it. As soon as man was cast out of Paradise, God set up, "the cherubim and the fiery sword that turns about to keep the way of the tree of life" (Genesis 3:24). The cherubim were also mentioned many times when speaking of the tabernacle in the wilderness and the Old Testament temple.

An example of this is the picture of the cherubim shadowing the Ark of the Covenant, for the Lord says, "They shall be made, one cherub on this side, and another cherub on the other side of the mercy seat; and you shall make the two cherubim on the two sides. The cherubim shall stretch forth their wings above, overshadowing the mercy seat with their wings; and their faces shall be toward each other, the faces of the cherubim shall be toward the mercy seat. And you shall set the mercy seat on the ark above, and you shall put into the ark the testimonies which I shall give you. And I will make Myself known to you from there, and I will speak to you from above the mercy seat between the two cherubim, which are upon the Ark of Testimony, even in all things which I shall charge you concerning the children of Israel" (Exodus 25:19–22).

This means that God used to speak to them by means

of the cherubim. In this way, the information the people used to take from God directly, they heard it from the cherubim, whose name means "full of knowledge." The drawing of the Cherubim was inserted in most of the engravings in the temples of old. This host's name is closely linked to God to the extent that the Psalmist said in his Psalms about God, "the One who sits on the cherubim" and "He rode on the cherubim and flew."

As we have previously explained, Satan himself was one of the host of the cherubim, which means, "full of knowledge." This may reveal to us how Satan met his downfall. Knowledge alone puffs up if separated from God. It is turned into arrogance in knowledge and science, which leads its owner to downfall. This is why St. Paul the apostle says, "Knowledge puffs up" (1 Corinthians 8:1).

Some people relate the cherubim to the four incorporeal creatures, because the qualities mentioned of them in Revelations 4:6–9 are the same qualities attributed to the cherubim. Likewise, the praise ritual is attributed to the cherubim also, just as the seraphim. This is why the church prays in the holy liturgy, "You are He around whom the cherubim stand, and the seraphim of six wings constantly praising You, non-ceasing saying, 'Holy, Holy, Holy the Lord of Hosts, heaven and earth are full of Your holy glory."

(3) The Seats or the Thrones. This is an exalted host among the sublime heavenly hosts about whom we do not know much. These are mentioned in the liturgy of St. Gregory the theologian. "You are He to whom the thrones send up honor, thousands and thousands stand

before You, and myriads of myriads offer You service." It seems that the work for all of these is to praise God.

b. The Second Host or Category: the Lords, the Authorities, the Dominions and the Powers. It seems that all of these have a job to praise God and to glorify Him and to present what is appropriate and honorable to Him.

The Liturgy of St. Basil says, "Before whom stand the angels, the archangels, the authorities, the thrones, the thrones, the dominions, and the powers."

In the Liturgy of St. Gregory, it says, "You are He whom the angels praise and the archangels worship. You are He whom the principalities bless and to whom the dominions cry. You are He whose glory the authorities declare. You are He unto whom the thrones send up the honor. Thousands and thousands stand before You, and ten thousands times ten thousands offer You service."

Contemplate on this: the authorities, the lords, the dominions, the thrones, thousands and thousands, endless multitudes, all of them praise God and glorify Him and offer Him honor.

c. The Third Category of the Heavenly Hosts: the Angels and the Archangels. The ordinary angels seem to be the least of the heavenly ranks and their job is to serve humans. As for the archangels, the Jewish tradition makes the number of the archangels seven. Among them is Michael, Gabriel and Raphael: these three are the most famous.

(1) Archangel Michael: the word Michael consists of three syllables: Mi-cha-el, meaning "He who is like God." It is mentioned in Daniel 10:13 that "one of the princes." Daniel speaks of him as the angel whom God has assigned to keep watch over His people, and to defend their interests. "At that time Michael the great prince shall stand up, that stands over the children of your people" (Daniel 12:1). Jude the apostle, also mentioned him in his epistle "Yet Michael the archangel, in contending with the devil, when he disputed about the body of Moses, dared not bring against him a reviling accusation, but said, 'The Lord rebuke you!'" (Jude 1:9).

(2) Archangel Gabriel: his name consists of two syllables: "Gabr," meaning "strong;" and "iel" meaning "God." Thus the name Gabriel means God's strong one or God's strength. We read about him in the annunciation of the nativity of St. John the Baptist and also in the annunciation of the Virgin, the Mother of Light, St. Mary, telling her of the birth of the Lord Jesus. It is Gabriel who addressed Zechariah saying, "The angel answered and said to him 'I am Gabriel, who stands in the presence of God, and was sent to speak to you and bring you these glad tidings'" (Luke 1:19). From this point, Gabriel has been called the Angel of the good news of annunciation.

(3) Archangel Raphael: the meaning of his name is, "God's healing" or "God's mercy." Some say the meaning of his name is "the rejoicer of the hearts." We read about

him in the book of Tobit. Archangel Raphael was sent to Tobit, saved him and was able to perform healing.

Guardian Angels

Our blessed church believes every man has a guardian angel. This is supported by the Lord Jesus' words concerning the little children, "Take heed that you do not despise one of these little ones, for I say to you that in heaven their angels always see the face of My Father who is in heaven" (Matthew 18:10). Likewise is the story of St. Peter the apostle when in jail, as mentioned in Acts 12. After leaving jail, he went to where the believers were gathered, praying for his sake. When knocking on the door, the maid Rhoda recognized his voice without opening the door. When she went in and told those gathered, they could not believe her, and said, "It is his angel" (Acts 12:15). This belief is the same one that the Jews believe in; that every person has his guardian angel. The conclusion is that the angels' position in the New Testament is clearer than that of the Old Testament. In addition, their manifestation is greater in number. This is not surprising, because the angels are spirits assigned to serve those who will surely inherit the salvation fulfilled by Christ Jesus on the Cross.

5

Death and the Afterlife

What happens after death? What shall we do in heaven? This is a serious and important topic, because it concerns us in the first place due to its link to our eternal future. Our current life is only a preparation for the life to come. What man sows, he reaps. Man plants here on earth and reaps up in heaven.

Every Man Must Die

Whenever we mention death, some of us recoil and get pessimistic. Actually, this is an escape from reality and shows our lack of true faith. Let us be practical and believing. Death is an issue that prevails over and includes everyone. The Psalmist asks in amazement, "What man is there who shall live, and not see death? Shall anyone deliver his soul from the hand of Hades?" (88:48). The same concept is confirmed by Saint Paul the Apostle when he says, "And as it is appointed for men to die once, but after this the judgment" (Hebrews 9:27).

As far as we know, no man has escaped death. Even the two who ascended to heaven alive—the righteous Enoch and Elijah the prophet (Genesis 5:24; 2 Kings 2:9–11)—will return to our world at the end of times, before Christ's Second Coming and will taste death as two martyrs. This is based on what is mentioned in Revelation 11:3–9.

The Concept of Death in Christianity

Death is the end of a painful stage in man's life in a world of toil and affliction. It is also a beginning of an eternal life full of joy. The Lord Jesus, glory be to Him, tasted death willingly and changed it to life! Therefore, Christianity looks to death as victory and conquest. Saint Paul the apostle speaks of death and the rising of the bodies for an entire chapter (1 Corinthians 15). He says, "But thanks be to God, who gives us the victory through our Lord Jesus Christ" (1 Corinthians 15:57). We believe that Christ ". . . has abolished death and brought life and immortality to light through the gospel" (2 Timothy 1:10). Before Christ, death was a thorn, and Christ has broken it, and even plucked it out of the human heart. "O Death, where is your sting? O Hades, where is your victory" (1 Corinthians 15:55). For death is not the end to our existence; rather, it is the entrance to a more perfect and a more sublime life than that on earth. "For we know that if our earthly house, this tent, is destroyed, we have a building from God, a house not made with hands, eternal in the heavens" (2 Corinthians 5:1).

The body is not everything in man; rather, he has a spirit that accompanies his body and dwells in him. This spirit is the mystery behind his life and action. As soon as the spirit departs from him, death occurs. If the Holy Book has made it explicit that God created man in His own image, this image and similarity concerns the soul and spirit and it does not concern the body, because "God is Spirit" (John 4:24; 2 Corinthians 3:17). Therefore, man's spirit is in the image of God—it is a free spirit, immortal, pure, sanctified, and has dominion over nature and all that is in nature.

However, man's spirit is limited, whereas God's spirit is boundless. This human spirit is the source of reason, and this is why it departs from man on his death. "All flesh would die together, and every mortal would return to the earth from where he was formed" (Job 34:15). This is why it was said of Abraham, Isaac, and Jacob that they gave up the spirit and died. Furthermore, Saint Stephen, the first martyr in Christianity, said at the moment of his death, "Lord Jesus, receive my spirit" (Acts 7:59).

In the Holy Book, there is a beautiful expression in which one asks that his/her spirit be committed or deposited into the hands of the Creator until the general judgment day. David the prophet said, "Into Your hands I commit my spirit" (Psalms 31:5). In the same way the Lord Jesus, to Him be the glory, committed His human spirit at His death on the Cross. This human soul is different than that of His divinity. "Father, into Your hands I commit My spirit.' Having said this, He breathed His last" (Luke 23:46).

The Soul and the Spirit

Before we plunge into tonight's topic, it is preferable that we contemplate a little on two words: the spirit and the soul. We often confuse the two together in our expressions. They are even analogized quite often in the Holy Book. So, what is the difference between the soul and the spirit?

The word "spirit" refers to the rational and non-material essence—the immortal element in man. We know the existence of the spirit from the outer traces of the spirit. However, the "soul" refers to the live essence or the vital strength in the living being.

In all of the old and the new languages, there is a different word for the "soul" and the "spirit." In the Greek language, the spirit is *pnevma*, whereas the soul is *psee*. In Hebrew we find the spirit as *ruah*, whereas the soul is *nephesh*. This is similar to the Arabic, which uses the word *rooh* for spirit and *nafs* for soul. The ancient Egyptians discerned the soul from the spirit by using the word *ba* to express the spirit and the word *ka* to express the soul. In French, *esprit* is used to express the spirit and *name* to express the soul. This usage of the spirit and the soul is found in the holy books as well as in the books of philosophy. But sometimes we find the word soul used in the holy books to express the spirit.

Those Who Deny the Resurrection of the Body

Since the olden times, there have been those who deny the resurrection of the body, including philosophers, atheists, and those among the Jews themselves. When they deny the resurrection of the body, they also deny the doctrine of the general resurrection at the end of times.

Among those who denied the resurrection of the body before Christianity were the Epicurean philosophers who boldly declared their materialistic tendency and their rejection of religion. The motto for their philosophy was, "Let us eat and drink and be merry, for tomorrow we die." To this material attitude Saint Paul the apostle referred in his first epistle to the Corinthians, and he adopted the Epicurean philosophic motto, saying, "If the dead do not rise, 'Let us eat and drink, for tomorrow we die!'" (15:32).

Following the Epicurean footsteps in denying the resurrection of the body, came the Stoic philosophy, the followers of the Greek philosopher Xenon. The Stoics taught that the spirits, after they leave the bodies, return to the greatest god, who is the origin and there the spirits decease in him. Therefore, they said, there was no need for any resurrection. Saint Paul the Apostle met with some of these Epicurean and Stoic philosophers in the city of Athens. As he was preaching to them the Lord Jesus, they were saying among themselves, "What does this babbler want to say?" As soon as he began to tell them of the resurrection from the dead, they began to mock him (Acts 17:18, 32).

Regarding the principles of these people, the writer of the book of Wisdom of Solomon says, "For they reasoned unsoundly saying to themselves, 'Short and sorrowful is our life, and there is no remedy when a life comes to its end, and no one has been know to return from Hades. For we were born by mere chance, and hereafter we shall be as though we had never been, for the breath in our nostrils is smoke, and reason is a spark kindled by the beating of our hearts; when it is extinguished, the body will turn to ashes, and the spirit will dissolve like empty air. Our nature will be forgotten in time, and no one will remember our works; our life will pass away like the traces of a cloud and be scattered like mist that is chased by the rays of the sun and overcome by its heat. For our allotted time is the passing of a shadow, and there is no return from our death, because it is sealed up and no one turns back. Come, therefore, let us enjoy the good things that exist, and make use of the creation to the full as in youth'" (2:1–6). It is clear from these verses they are the same concepts as those of the Stoics and Epicureans. However, the wise Solomon denounces them later on and says, "Thus they reasoned, but they were led astray, for their wickedness blinded, them, and they did not know the secret purposes of God, nor hoped for the wages of holiness, nor discerned the prize for blameless souls; for God created us for incorruption, and made us in the image of His own eternity" (2:21–23).

We might not be surprised if these are the beliefs of some of the atheist philosophers. But, what is truly amazing is to find a large Jewish sect, the Sadducees (and many other Jewish priests and chief- priests who belonged to the sect of the Sadducees), deny the resurrection of the flesh and the immortality of the soul. Moreover, they denied the existence of the spirits and angels. Saint Matthew the Evangelist, refers to the corrupt "Sadducees, who say there is no resurrection" (22:23). In addition, the writer of the book of Acts refers to them and says, "For Sadducees say that there is no resurrection, and no angel or spirit" (23:8).

How did these corrupt doctrines spread to them? The Sadducees had a traditional animosity against the Scribes and Pharisees who resisted anything foreign and called for the strict commitment to the old law, whether written or oral. With this attitude, they were contrary to the Sadducees who were connected with the Gentiles and adopted their Hellenic, or Greek, culture. As a result, the scribes and the Pharisees scorned the Sadducees and considered them deserters to the essence of Moses' old law.

However, the Sadducees, scribes and Pharisees were not the only ones who denied the immortality of the soul and the resurrection of the body before the dawn of Christianity. In fact, some Christian heretics at the beginning of Christianity also denied these doctrines. Among these were the followers of Simon, the Samaritan magician, and Mina Nadr, Kabokrat, Marcion and the Agnostics.

In the modern age, those who lead the campaign against the immortality of the soul and the resurrection of the body are those who are materialistic, rationalistic and ignorant. Those who have denied the existence of the soul, have they immortalized it. Others say that the resurrection is preposterous and untenable!

The Resurrection From the Dead in the Holy Scriptures

We have previously mentioned in the first and the second topics of this chain a number of proofs, whether from the Holy Books or from other sources, about man's immortality and eternal life. Today, concerning this subject, we attempt to prove the truth of the resurrection of the dead. The evidence about the soul's immortality without the divine inspiration could never give us a clear picture that is perfect about this subject.

1. In the Old Testament

In the Old Testament we find transient references about the resurrection from among the dead. We also find practical evidence about this truth:

For instance, we find Isaiah the prophet saying, "The dead shall rise, and those that are in the tombs shall be raised up, and those that are in the earth shall rejoice" (26:19). Daniel the prophet, moreover, says "Many of them that sleep in the dust of the earth shall awake, some to everlasting life, and some to reproach and everlasting shame" (12:2).

In the second book of Maccabees, we find a man telling the king who was tormenting him because he would not defile God's law: "And when he was at his last breath, he said, 'You accursed wretch, you dismiss us from this present life, but the King of the universe will raise us up to an everlasting renewal of life, because we have died for His laws'" (7:9).

In addition to the words of the divine inspiration, the Old Testament records to us three cases that are practical evidence about the resurrection from among the dead. We mean by this: the raising of the widow's son in Sidom, whom Elijah the prophet raised (1 Kings 17); also the Shunammite woman's son whom Elisha the prophet raised from the dead (2 Kings 4:34–37); and the man who was raised from the dead when he touched the bones of Elisha the prophet (2 Kings 13:20–21).

2. In the New Testament

As for the New Testament, we find the resurrection crowning the redeeming work of God's Son. It is the cornerstone of Christianity as a religion. The resurrection creed is related to Christ's own resurrection from the dead, to the extent that Saint Paul the apostle said, "If there is no resurrection of the dead, then Christ is not risen. And if Christ is not risen, then our preaching is empty and your faith is also empty" (1 Corinthians 15:13–14).

The teaching of the resurrection from among the dead is as clear as could be as taught by the Lord Jesus Himself and His deeds. He said, to Him be the glory, "Do not marvel at this; for the hour is coming in which all who are in the graves will hear His voice and come forth—those who have done good, to the resurrection of life, and those who have done evil, to the resurrection of condemnation

(John 5:28–29).

He also overcomes the Sadducees who deny the resurrection, by his words, "But concerning the resurrection of the dead, have you not read what was spoken to you by God, saying, 'I am the God of Abraham, the God of Isaac, and the God of Jacob? God is not the God of the dead, but of the living'" (Matthew 22:31–32).

The Lord also said to one of those who invited him to eat, "But when you give a feast, invite the poor, the maimed, the lame, the blind. And you will be blessed, because they cannot repay you; for you shall be repaid at the resurrection of the just" (Luke 14:13–14).

He also told the scribes and the Pharisees once, "The men of Nineveh will rise up in the judgment with this generation and condemn it, because they repented at the preaching of Jonah; and indeed a greater than Jonah is here. The queen of the South will rise up in the judgment with this generation and condemn it, for she came from the ends of the earth to hear the wisdom of Solomon; and indeed a greater than Solomon is here" (Matthew 12:41–42).

If we look at Saint Paul the Apostle, we shall find him declaring openly the resurrection reality before the Sanhedrin council, which is the Jewish high council, saying, "Concerning the hope and resurrection of the dead I am being judged!" (Acts 23:6). Before Felix, the Roman ruler, he said, "I have hope in God, which they themselves also accept, that there will be a resurrection of the dead, both of the just and the unjust" (Acts 24:15). Saint Paul the apostle once more confirmed this meaning before the Jewish king Agrippa, and he said, "To this day

I stand, witnessing both to small and great, saying no other things than those which the prophets and Moses said would come—that the Christ would suffer, that He would be the first to rise from the dead, and would proclaim light to the Jewish people and to the Gentiles" (Acts 26:22–23). Moreover, Saint Paul devoted an entire chapter to the resurrection, which is Chapter 15 of his first epistle to Corinth. He was defending the creed of the resurrection of the dead and answering the attacks of the cult of heretics (which we shall later discuss). In addition, he has written other epistles where he defends the creed of the resurrection.

As for Saint Peter, he writes in warning of the heretics who were the enemies of the resurrection creed, saying, "Knowing this first: that scoffers will come in the last days, walking according to their own lusts, and saying, 'Where is the promise of His coming? For since the fathers fell asleep, all things continue as they were from the beginning of creation'...The Lord is not slack concerning His promise, as some count slackness, but is longsuffering toward us, not willing that any should perish but that all should come to repentance. But the day of the Lord will come as a thief in the night, in which the heavens will pass away with a great noise, and the elements will melt with fervent heat; both the earth and the works that are in it will be burned up...Nevertheless we, according to His promise, look for new heavens and a new earth in which righteousness dwells...You therefore, beloved, since you know this beforehand, beware lest you also fall from your own steadfastness, being led away with the error of the wicked" (2 Peter 3:3, 4, 9, 10, 13, 17).

In the New Testament, in a clearer way than in the Old Testament, we can see the Lord Jesus supporting the resurrection creed with practical miracles to many whom He has raised from among the dead. The holy gospels did not mention except three cases of the dead that the Lord Jesus raised. This has a godly meaning in addition to its spiritual meaning. These three cases are Jarius' daughter, the widow's son in Nain and Lazarus whom the Lord raised from the grave after his body had rotted as a result of being in the grave for four days.

Furthermore, in the New Testament, it has been mentioned that many of those who were dead, rose from among the dead. For example:

The many saints that came out of their graves after the Lord Jesus committed His Spirit into the Father's hands. These entered Jerusalem: "The graves were opened; and many bodies of the saints who had fallen asleep were raised; and coming out of the graves after His resurrection, they went into the holy city and appeared to many" (Matthew 27:52–53). The church tradition mentions the number of those who died and rose from among the dead as five hundred! When the Lord Jesus cried out in a loud voice, these arose and gathered at the Mount of Olives. Because of the Lord's glorious resurrection, they entered the blessed city of Jerusalem and they appeared to many!

Tabitha, whom Saint Peter the apostle raised after she had died in the city of Java (Acts 9:36–42).

The young man Eutychus whom Saint Paul the apostle brought back to life after he fell from the third floor in the city of Troas in Asia Minor, when Saint Paul was preaching an elaborate sermon (Acts 20:7–12).

The appearance of the two prophets Moses and Elijah together with the Lord Jesus on the Mountain of Transfiguration, approximately fifteen hundred years after the death of the former, and nine hundred years after the latter's live ascension to heaven.

The creed of the resurrection from among the dead is a well-founded creed in our Christian faith. The apostles and the fathers stated in the creed of the faith they have set that it must be studied by every person who desires to be baptized. The catechumen is to declare that creed of the faith at the time of his or her baptism as a commitment to the correct faith. Saint Paul the apostle merely referred the scholars to this creed of faith by saying, "Therefore, leaving the discussion of the elementary principles of Christ, let us go on to perfection, not laying again the foundation of repentance from dead works and of faith toward God, of the doctrine of baptisms, of laying on of hands, of resurrection of the dead, and of eternal judgment" (Hebrews 6:1–2).

The creed of the faith set by the apostles was the seed of the creed of faith set by the fathers assembled in the universal assemblies: the first council in 325 AD at Nicea and the second council in 381 AD at Constantinople. In this creed, we admit and proclaim our own faith: "We look for the resurrection of the dead, and the life of the age to come." Based on great wisdom, the Church chants openly this same piece before beginning the Prayer of Reconciliation in the Divine Liturgy. By doing so, the Church desires to instill this creed deep into the hearts of Her believers.

The Creed of the resurrection of the bodies has

been explained and confirmed by many of the apostolic fathers, some of who were the disciples of the twelve disciples of Christ. Among these is Saint Clement, the bishop of Rome, who lived at the end of the first century. In a letter to the church of Corinth, he wrote "I wish, dear brethren, that we take into consideration how that the Lord constantly assures and proves to us that there will be the resurrection in the future, of which the Lord Jesus was the prime." In addition, Saint Polycarp—the martyr, bishop of Smyrna and disciple of Saint John the Apostle—says in his letter to the church at Philippi, "He who does not confess the testimony of the Cross, is from Satan. Anyone who twists the words of the Lord for the sake of his passions, and says there is no resurrection or judgment, then he is the prime of Satan." Saint Justin the martyr and the philosopher who lived at the end of the first century and the beginning of the second, wrote a book about the resurrection of the dead. This has been mostly lost, and time has only preserved for us a few bits that contain ten short chapters.

In this way, it is obvious to us that the Christian belief in the immortality of the soul and the resurrection of the bodies is a well-founded creed as much as the other cornerstones of the Christian faith.

3. In the Writings of Saint Paul the Apostle

Of all the beautiful writings about the truth of the resurrection of the bodies in the New Testament, what Saint Paul the apostle, the teacher, wrote is perhaps the most beautiful of all. In Chapter 15 of his first epistle to the Corinth church, Saint Paul clarifies the creed of the resurrection, referring to it strongly by good evidence. He warns us of the new heretics who deny it and answers the questions provoked concerning it at this early time. Saint Paul the Apostle tackled these issues surrounding the creed of the resurrection in an epistle he wrote to the church in Greece, a place which was considered to be the cradle of philosophy. Surely, this was in response to the influence of the Roman and Epicurean philosophy that denied the resurrection of the body. These philosophical trends prevailed in this country, and thus he writes in this fashion, "Now if Christ is preached that He has been raised from the dead, how do some among you say that there is no resurrection of the dead?" (15:12).

Saint Paul the apostle set the evidence of the truth concerning the resurrection of the bodies by the following proofs:

Christ's resurrection that is assuredly proclaimed by His manifestations and appearances: "For I delivered to you first of all that which I also received: that Christ died for our sins according to the Scriptures, and that He was buried, and that He rose again the third day according to the Scriptures, and that He was seen by Cephas, then by the twelve. After that He was seen by over five hundred brethren at once, of whom the greater part remain to the present, but some have fallen asleep. After that He was seen by James, then by all the apostles. Then last of all He was seen by me also, as by one born out of due time" (1 Corinthians 15:3–8).

The apostles' effective preaching concerning the

resurrection: "Now if Christ is preached that He has been raised from the dead, how do some among you say that there is no resurrection of the dead? But if there is no resurrection of the dead, then Christ is not risen. And if Christ is not risen, then our preaching is empty and your faith is also empty" (1 Corinthians 15:12–14).

The faith and hope of the Christians who rely on this foundation. "Yes, and we are found false witnesses of God, because we have testified of God that He raised up Christ, whom He did not raise up—if in fact the dead do not rise. For if the dead do not rise, then Christ is not risen. And if Christ is not risen, your faith is futile; you are still in your sins! Then also those who have fallen asleep in Christ have perished. If in this life only we have hope in Christ, we are of all men the most pitiable. But now Christ is risen from the dead, and has become the firstfruits of those who have fallen asleep" (1 Corinthians 15:15–20).

The encounter between Adam who made us inherit death and Christ the second Adam who granted us life and makes us live. "For since by man came death, by Man also came the resurrection of the dead. For as in Adam all die, even so in Christ all shall be made alive" (1 Corinthians 15:21–22).

The Christian people's attitude in asking for God's mercy towards their dead. "Otherwise, what will they do who are baptized for the dead, if the dead do not rise at all? Why then are they baptized for the dead?" (1 Corinthians 15:29).

How the apostles endangered their life even unto death, in expectation of the promise for life eternal. "If the dead do not rise at all...why do we stand in jeopardy every hour?... If the dead do not rise, 'Let us eat and drink, for tomorrow we die!'" (1 Corinthians 15:29–32).

Then Saint Paul speaks of the concepts of the new cults after he has summarized them in two points:

The resurrection is impossible due to the bodies' disintegration. Here the apostle offers an example of the plant that does not live unless it dies. "But someone will say, 'How are the dead raised up? And with what body do they come?' Foolish one, what you sow is not made alive unless it dies. And what you sow, you do not sow that body that shall be, but mere grain—perhaps wheat or some other grain. But God gives it a body as He pleases, and to each seed its own body" (1 Corinthians 15:35–38).

Regarding the kind of body in which man is raised. It is here that the apostle answers that our own bodies are the ones that change amazingly, but still keeping the essential unit. "But God gives it a body as He pleases, and to each seed its own body. All flesh is not the same flesh, but there is one kind of flesh of men, another flesh of animals, another of fish, and another of birds. There are also celestial bodies and terrestrial bodies; but the glory of the celestial is one, and the glory of the terrestrial is another. There is one glory of the sun, another glory of the moon, and another glory of the stars; for one star differs from another star in glory. So also is the resurrection of the dead. The body is sown in corruption, it is raised in incorruption. It is sown in dishonor, it is raised in glory. It is sown in weakness, it is raised in power. It is sown a natural body, it is raised a spiritual body. There is a natural body, and there is a spiritual body. And so it is written, 'The first man Adam became a living being.' The last Adam became a life-giving spirit. However, the spiritual is not first, but the natural, and afterward the spiritual. The first man was of the earth, made of dust; the second Man is the Lord from heaven. As was the man of dust, so also are those who are made of dust; and as is the heavenly Man, so also are those who are heavenly. And as we have borne the image of the man of dust, we shall also bear the image of the heavenly Man. Now this I say, brethren, that flesh and blood cannot inherit the kingdom of God; nor does corruption inherit incorruption" (1 Corinthians 15:38–50).

Again Saint Paul the Apostle in his second epistle to the Corinthians confirms the reality of the resurrection from the dead: "knowing that He who raised up the Lord Jesus will also raise us up with Jesus, and will present us with you" (2 Corinthians 4:14). "For we must all appear before the judgment seat of Christ, that each one may receive the things done in the body, according to what he has done, whether good or bad" (2 Corinthians 5:10). "For we know that if our earthly house, this tent, is destroyed, we have a building from God, a house not made with hands, eternal in the heavens. For in this we groan, earnestly desiring to be clothed with our habitation which is from heaven, if indeed, having been clothed, we shall not be found naked. For we who are in this tent groan, being burdened, not because we want to be unclothed, but further clothed, that mortality may be swallowed up by life" (2 Corinthians 5:1–4).

In the epistle to the Philippians, Saint Paul considers the resurrection from the dead to be his hope. He therefore says, "that I may know Him and the power of His resurrection, and the fellowship of His sufferings, being conformed to His death, if, by any means, I may attain to the resurrection from the dead" (3:10–11).

In his second epistle to Timothy, which he wrote during his second imprisonment in Rome, when he was a few steps away from his death, he says, "This is a faithful saying: For if we died with Him, We shall also live with Him. If we endure, We shall also reign with Him. If we deny Him, He also will deny us" (2:11–12).

What Happens to Man After Death?

Many ask, "What happens to man after death?" When man dies, his spirit is separated from his body and so he becomes a dead corpse, and soon enough this body has no value whatsoever. He returns to the dust from which he came, but as for the spirit, this returns to God. But what happens to the spirit? There are different opinions that answer this question, and we hereby mention some of them:

1. A Heretical Opinion

One opinion is that the spirits of the people will sleep until the judgment day, both the righteous and the evil ones. This is also the opinion of the heretics, including the Seventh day Adventists. Where did they get this opinion from? They base this wrong opinion on the condemnation and judgment on the resurrection day. Death has often been called in the Holy Book "sleep" or "laying down to rest" as the Lord Jesus spoke of Lazarus, "Our friend Lazarus sleeps, but I go that I may wake him up" (John 11:11). He also said concerning the daughter of Jairus, "the girl is not dead, but sleeping" (Matthew 9:24). However, this opinion is wrong for the following reasons:

The story of the rich man and Lazarus is a very important story found in Luke 16. The Lord Jesus says that the poor one died and was carried by the angels to Abraham's embrace, whereas the rich one also died and was buried. When the rich man went to Hades he lifted up his eyes...etc. What does this mean? Were they in Hades or in Abraham's embrace, sleeping? Certainly not. Although they claim that this story is only symbolic, we believe that this could not be used just as a symbol, because when the Lord Jesus uses such an analogy, then there is no absolute similarity between the one referred to and the referral himself, as the well known basic facts state.

The Lord Jesus, to Him be the glory, said to the thief on the right on the Cross, "Today you will be with Me in Paradise" (Luke 23:43). The Lord did not say, "Today you will be with Me in sleep."

When Saint Paul the apostle says, "Having a desire to depart and be with Christ, which is far better" (Philippians 1:23), this "far better" that the apostle is eager for could not possibly be a mere long sleep! If Saint Paul the apostle's desire was for a long sleep, this would have been just an escape from serving Christ due to the dangers and the toil of this service—a service in which Saint Paul was needed. This is exactly what we understand from Saint Paul the apostle's words, "So we are always confident, knowing that while we are at home in the body we are absent from the Lord. For we walk by faith, not by sight. We are confident, yes, well pleased rather to be absent from the body and to be present with the Lord" (2 Corinthians 5:6–8). From these words is it clear that we shall dwell with the Lord, and that we shall not sleep!

Saint Stephen the Archdeacon and Protomartyr, says in his last breath, "Lord Jesus, receive my spirit" (Acts 7:59). The issue to him was not a matter of sleep, neither was it to show martyrs who gave their life for the Lord's sake. Furthermore, there were those whom Saint John saw in his divine revelation saying, "How long, O Lord, holy and true, until You judge and avenge our blood on those who dwell on the earth?" (Revelations 6:9–11). The answer was, "Then a white robe was given to each of them; and it was said to them that they should rest a little while longer, until both the number of their fellow servants and their brethren, who would be killed as they were, was completed." Therefore, the martyrs are not asleep as claimed by this corrupt opinion that the heretics have adopted.

2. The Opinion of Judgment Immediately After Death

An opinion adopted by the Roman Catholic Church says that there is a special judgment straight after death.

But our Coptic Orthodox Church teaches us there is no special judgment directly after death, and that the absolute recompense for the righteous and the wicked will be only after the general judgment for all mankind. There are many proofs to support this belief:

The words of the Lord Jesus in the parable of the wheat and the tares (Matthew 13:24, 30, 36, 43). This is a symbolic parable for the wicked and the righteous. When this lord's laborers ask him to allow them to uproot the weeds, he refuses and tells them, "No, lest while gather up the tares you also uproot the wheat with them. Let both grow together until the harvest, and at the time of harvest I will say to the reapers, 'First gather together the tares and bind them in bundles to burn them, but gather the wheat into my barn.'" The Lord Jesus has explained this parable Himself and said, "Therefore as the tares are gathered and burned in the fire, so it will be at the end of this age. The Son of Man will send out His angels, and they will gather out of His kingdom all things that offend, and those who practice lawlessness, and will cast them into the furnace of fire." The important question is this: when will this be? "At the end of the age" and not before then.

The parable of the ten virgins, the wise and the foolish ones (Matthew 25:1–13). This is an image of the Second Advent and the judgment. The special judgment then does not go in accordance with this clear picture in the parable: "But while the bridegroom was delayed, they all slumbered and slept. And at midnight a cry was heard: 'Behold, the bridegroom is coming; go out to meet him!' Then all those virgins arose and trimmed their lamps. And the foolish said to the wise, 'Give us some of your oil, for our lamps are going out.' But the wise answered, saying, 'No, lest there should not be enough for us and you; but go rather to those who sell, and buy for yourselves.' And while they went to buy, the bridegroom came, and those who were ready went in with him to the wedding; and the door was shut. Afterward the other virgins came also, saying 'Lord, Lord, open to us!' But he answered and said, 'Assuredly, I say to you, I do not know you.'" Therefore, we do not find any reference, be it from far or near, to any special judgment.

The words of the Lord Jesus about His Second Advent (Matthew 25:31–46): "When the Son of Man comes in His glory, and all the holy angels with Him, then He will sit on the throne of His glory. All the nations will be gathered before Him, and He will separate them one from another, as a shepherd divides his sheep from the goats. And He will set the sheep on His right hand, but the goats on the left." Here too there is no mention of any special judgment, unless it is in the general common judgment for all mankind.

From what is mentioned in the epistles of Saint Paul the apostle in various situations, such as:

(1) In his second epistle to the Thessalonians, he says, "Since it is a righteous thing with God to repay with tribulation those who trouble you, and to give you who are troubled rest with us when the Lord Jesus is revealed from heaven with His mighty angels, in flaming fire taking vengeance on those who do not know God, and on those who do not obey the gospel of our Lord Jesus Christ"

(1:6–8). So, when will the believers take their rest? They will take it when the Lord Jesus is declared and manifested from heaven, that is, on the Judgment Day.

(2) In his epistle to the Hebrews, after the apostle spoke of the righteous and the saints in the Old Testament, he says, "And all these, having obtained a good testimony through faith, did not receive the promise, God having provided something better for us, that they should not be made perfect apart from us" (11:39–40). For, they will not continue without us in the other world. This means that the judgment for everyone will be together.

From the parable of the slaves and the talents (Matthew 25:14–30). In this parable the Lord Jesus speaks of a man who has traveled, given his laborers talents and left. After a long time, the master came back and wanted to see the account. From the parable it is clear that He was speaking of the last judgment, and yet, there is no reference to any special judgment.

In his second epistle to Timothy, Saint Paul asserts the issue of the general judgment, when he was on the verge of his death saying, "For I am already being poured out as a drink offering, and the time of my departure is at hand. I have fought the good fight, I have finished the race, I have kept the faith. Finally, there is laid up for me the crown of righteousness, which the Lord, the righteous Judge, will give to me on that Day, and not to me only but also to all who have loved His appearing" (4:6–8). Thus, the recompense day is one—whether it is for Saint Paul or for all believers.

Saint Paul the apostle also calls the judgment day the

day of wrath. He says, "But in accordance with your hardness and your impenitent heart you are treasuring up for yourself wrath in the day of wrath and revelation of the righteous judgment of God" (Romans 2:5). It is the one day, common and general to all people.

From Saint Peter the apostle's speech addressed to the priests. "The elders who are among you I exhort, I who am a fellow elder and a witness of the sufferings of Christ, and also a partaker of the glory that will be revealed: Shepherd the flock of God which is among you, serving as overseers, not by compulsion but willingly, not for dishonest gain but eagerly; nor as being lords over those entrusted to you, but being examples to the flock; and when the Chief Shepherd appears, you will receive the crown of glory that does not fade away" (1 Peter 5:1–4). It is obvious that the Lord Jesus, the chief Shepherd, when He will appear in His Second Advent, so full of glory, will give the crown of glory.

The word of decision in this issue is that of the Lord Jesus, to Him be the glory. He says, "He who rejects Me, and does not receive My words, has that which judges him—the word that I have spoken will judge him in the last day" (John 12:48). Therefore, there is judgment for everyone on the last day. Thus, there is no reason behind those who say there is a special judgment.

3. The Opinion of Purgatory

Another opinion adopted by the Roman Catholic Church says that there is a place called "purgatory." This opinion, briefly speaking, says that the spirits of those who die in the Roman Catholic faith without repenting of their temporal sins according to the mystery of the Church's repentance law will go to purgatory, where their souls will be purified by the purification fire. They believe the torture in purgatory is that of the gray fire, having the purpose of purification and repentance. The period of time in purgatory is not a definite one; it differs from one person to the other according to his/her sins. It is possible to shorten or to alleviate the purgatory torture by means of prayer. This is considered to be the right of the church papal leaders, who alone have the right to do this by means of the saints' prayers. In such a situation, the righteousness of those saints relieves the torture. To interpret this, they believe the saints have struggled and achieved virtues much more than what God has asked of them. They believe these bonus saintly virtues have been centralized in the Pope, for he is a representative of Christ on earth. He alone has the right to grant it to whomever he wishes.

The Orthodox Church does not accept the doctrine of purgatory, and neither is it accepted by the Protestants. First of all, this doctrine is purely modern and the Christian Church has not known it since the Church was established. We do not find any indication or explanation for it from the period of Christ's death up until the seventh century. Rather, the first Catholic assembly to discuss it was the Council of Florence in 1439 and it was not accepted as a doctrine of the Roman Catholic faith until the assembly of Tridentate in 1445. Therefore, it is considered a newly intervening creed. This creed does not need much of an effort to prove its annulment.

From the parable of the rich man and Lazarus in Luke 16:19–31. In this parable, we find Lazarus has died and has been carried by the angels to Abraham's bosom, whereas the rich one also has died and was buried. The rich man lifted up his eyes when he was in Hades, the place where the evil ones await the general judgment in torture. "He lifted up his eyes and saw Abraham afar off, and Lazarus in his bosom. Then he cried and said, 'Father Abraham, have mercy on me, and send Lazarus that he may dip the tip of his finger in water and cool my tongue; for I am tormented in this flame.' But Abraham said, 'Son, remember that in your lifetime you received your good things, and likewise Lazarus evil things; but now he is comforted and you are tormented. And besides all this, between us and you there is a great gulf fixed, so that those who want to pass from here to you cannot, nor can those from there pass to us.'" This means there are only two places: one is a place of waiting for the righteous, and the other is the place of waiting for the evil ones, until the general judgment. There is no third place, in between the two, as is the claim of purgatory!

The purgatory creed contradicts the Lord's words, to Him be the glory, and His promise to the thief on the right, when Christ was on the cross. When the thief confessed Christ's divinity, the Lord Jesus' promise to him was, "Assuredly, I say to you, today you will be with Me in Paradise" (Luke 23:43). Then how is it that the thief did not experience purgatory if there is such a thing? Christ transferred in one moment a killer, a murderer, to Paradise, after his feet were on the threshold of hell, and yet he did not pass by purgatory. How, then could it be said after all of this, that it is necessary for a purgatory stage so the souls can be purified? It has been explicitly proved in the clearest possible way that sincere repentance transfers, on the spot, a criminal from death to paradise.

The purgatory concept implies scorn to Christ's salvation and His blood. The saying that the righteous are in need of purgatory to purify them shows that the blood of Christ is not good enough for salvation, that there should be something else to complete it. They claim that this thing is purgatory, even though the Holy Book declares openly, "and the blood of Jesus Christ His Son cleanses us from all sin" (1 John 1:7). Moreover, Saint Paul the apostle says, "Therefore He is also able to save to the uttermost those who come to God through Him, since He always lives to make intercession for them" (Hebrews 7:25). So, is it possible that after all of this, someone comes to say Christ's blood is not enough for salvation? Is this rational? In addition to this, the book of Revelation conveys to us a true picture of whom He is who lives in heaven. The book records for us a new hymn that is sung by the heavenly, "And they sang a new song, saying: 'You are worthy to take the scroll, And to open its seals; For You were slain, And have redeemed us to God by Your blood Out of every tribe and tongue and people and nation, And have made us kings and priests to our God; And we shall reign on the earth'" (5:9–10). Therefore, Christ has been slaughtered and He purchased us to God by His blood.

The purgatory concept lessens the impact of the mystery of repentance in the Church. If the souls that have repented have to cross the purgatory fire, then of what use is repentance? The Lord Jesus binds salvation with repentance; He says, "I tell you, no; but unless you repent you will all likewise perish" (Luke 13:3). Are we then, going to perish if we repent to God? According to Christ's promise, definitely not. Are we then in need of the fire of purgatory?

4. The Orthodox Opinion: The Creed

Since ancient times, the Orthodox Church believes and teaches that those who have departed, whether righteous or wicked ones, are in a waiting stage after their death until the day of the general judgment. To explain this more, we say:

Before Christ's redemption that was fulfilled on the Cross, all those who died, whether righteous or evil ones, saints or sinners, were held by Satan and pushed into the abyss, which is also known as Hades. Both of these words mean hellfire.

"Sheol" is a Hebrew word, whereas "Hades" is the Greek translation. The two words express the place where the spirits of the departed enter. All of the spirits of the righteous—those of Abraham, Isaac, Jacob, David, and all the other prophets—used to go to hell. In Hades, also, were all the evil spirits. Christ, after dying on the wooden Cross, instantly went to Hades and released the souls of those saintly and righteous ones that were confined and had died in the hope of His coming and His salvation. It is for this reason that Saint Peter the apostle said, "For Christ also suffered once for sins, the just for the unjust, that He might bring us to God, being put to death in the flesh but made alive by the Spirit, by whom also He went and preached to the spirits in prison" (1 Peter 3:18–19).

About this, Saint Paul the apostle says, "Therefore He says: 'When He ascended on high, He led captivity captive, and gave gifts to men.' (Now this, "He ascended"—what does it mean but that He also first descended into the lower parts of the earth? He who descended is also the One who ascended far above all the heavens, that He might fill all things.)" (Ephesians 4:8–10). This same meaning is also expressed in the Divine Liturgy about Christ when the priest says, "He descended into Hades, through the Cross." Christ, therefore, has descended to free those righteous ones who were caught in the devil's hands.

Since Christ had fulfilled the redemption, man now goes to the waiting place after his death. He either waits in paradise, with the righteous, or in Hades (or hell), with the wicked. As for hellfire, it is the place of eternal torment for the wicked, just as the heavenly kingdom is the eternal joyful place.

But what is the evidence of this creed for the waiting time? There is much evidence for this, which we shall briefly speak of:

a. *Concerning the Righteous.* Saint John says in his Revelation, "When he opened the fifth seal, I saw under the altar the souls of those who had been slain for the word of God and for the testimony which they held. And they cried with a loud voice saying, 'How long, O Lord, holy and true, until You judge and avenge our blood on those who dwell on the earth?' Then a white robe was given to each of them; and it was said to them that they should rest a little while longer, until both the number of their fellow servants and their brethren, who would be killed as they were, was completed" (Revelation 6:9–11). The statement "to rest a little while longer" implies, "to wait."

We also read in the book of the Revelation, the book that speaks of the other world, "Then I heard a voice from heaven saying to me, 'Write: "Blessed are the dead who die in the Lord from now on."' 'Yes,' says the Spirit, 'that they may rest from their labors, and their works follow them'" (14:13). This means there is a place of rest or waiting and that there is no immediate judgment. As for the statement, "their deeds follow them," the original Greek and Coptic text show the future form. Thus the literal translation would be, "their deeds will follow them!" That is, their deeds will follow them in the judgment when its time comes. As for now, they are in a state of waiting.

b. Concerning the Wicked. As for those who are wicked, and as to their waiting place, Saint Peter the apostle says, "Then the Lord knows how to deliver the godly out of temptations and to reserve the unjust under punishment for the day of judgment" (2 Peter 2:9). The words, "to reserve the unjust," in the Greek text and the Coptic, are found to be "as for the unrighteous, they are kept to the judgment day to be punished." The wicked, therefore, are in a waiting place for the judgment.

The Waiting Place

We have mentioned that our Coptic Church believes in and teaches of the two waiting places:

The waiting place for the righteous is called Paradise, which is also expressed by Saint Paul the apostle as "the third heaven" (2 Corinthians 12:2–4). The waiting place for the wicked is called Hades or hell; in Greek, *haides*, and in Coptic *amen*, which means "the source or place of the free spirits."

Paradise: can we define a geographical place? The first time Paradise was mentioned in the Holy Book was in Genesis 2:8–15. It was also known as the Garden of Eden. There was also mentioned the names of four rivers as geographical boundaries to this Paradise. Where did the waiting place, the paradise for the righteous, go? There are three different views in the Church regarding paradise:

1. Three Views of Paradise and Hades

One view says that Paradise is that the place which is mentioned in the book of Genesis where Adam and Eve were before being expelled as a result of their sin of disobedience. It was once a place on Earth, but was then was lifted up to Heaven—the one called by Saint Paul as the third heaven.

Another view that says that paradise was in heaven

and is still there. A third point of view says that paradise was on earth, and is still on earth, but it is hidden from our eyes after it has adopted a special spirituality. It has taken on a spiritual existence that cannot be visible to, or even realized by, the physical eyes.

We cannot say which of the three views is more convincing than the other. It is a quite mysterious matter to us, as long as the divine inspiration did not explain or reveal more. Saint Paul the apostle said well and truthfully, "For now we see in a mirror, dimly, but then face to face. Now I know in part, but then I shall know just as I also am known" (1 Corinthians 13:12).

As for Hades, or the abyss, which is the place of waiting for the wicked ones, it is believed that based on the linguistic meaning of the word "abyss," it is a place under the earth.

They rely on this due to many verses in the Holy Book. For example, David the prophet says, "What many and great afflictions have You shown me! Yet You turned and revived me, and brought me again from the depths of the earth" (Psalms 70:20). Also, he says, "If I should go up to heaven, You are there: if I make my bed in Sheol behold, You are there" (Psalms 139:8, NKJV). We notice when David speaks of Sheol, he uses the words "make my bed." Solomon's words in the book of Proverbs say, "The thoughts of the wise are ways of life, that he may turn aside and escape from hell" (15:24). Also, when Isaiah speaks of Satan he says, "Hell from beneath is provoked to meet you...Your glory has come down to Hades...But now you shall go down to hell, even to the foundations of the earth!" (14:9–15).

Saint Paul the apostle writes to the Romans, "Do not say in your heart, 'Who will ascend into heaven?' (that is, to bring Christ down from above) or, 'Who will descend into the abyss?' (that is, to bring Christ up from the dead)" (10:6–7). Also he says, "Now this, "He ascended"—what does it mean but that He also first descended into the lower parts of the earth?" (Ephesians 4:9). Based on all of these testimonies, some believed the abyss, or Sheol, is in the core of the earth. But it is probably symbolic and pictorial. The reference to the abyss, or Sheol, as being under the earth refers to the fact that it is degraded and ugly, contrary to heaven that is so exalted and sublime.

2. What Do the Departed Do in the Waiting Place?

This question crosses the mind of so many. The destiny of each of them has been defined, and each one knows his end. This is similar to students who have completed the exam and are waiting for the results. The righteous in paradise are looking up to the heavenly kingdom. As for the wicked, we may draw the analogy they are like those sentenced to death, while they are in waiting in Sheol. They know their end, and are waiting in fearful worry of the horrible execution of the death sentence. The righteous are waiting for the eternal glory, whereas the wicked are waiting for the eternal torment. All are waiting until the fellow slaves on earth fulfill their task.

At this point, there is another question that crosses the mind of many: Do the spirits of those departed feel for us, we the living ones? Can they offer any service for the humans on earth?

Firstly, the departed ones surely feel for us. As soon as man gets rid of his body, he sees so many things.

As for the departed ones, being concerned about those on earth, the parable of the rich man and Lazarus, said by Christ, is probably the one that answers us plainly concerning this question. When the rich man failed in achieving his first request from our father Abraham for his own sake, we find him pleading with Abraham to send Lazarus to his five brothers to make them realize the real situation and how disastrous their destiny would be, so they would not wind up as grievously as he did. This shows clearly the concern this rich man had, after his death, for his brothers' destiny.

The saying that there are two churches, one as struggling on earth and the other as victorious in heaven, does not portray the actual fact. It is more correct to say that it is one church, where some of the members departed to heaven, whereas the rest are still striving in their physical life in this hard world.

If the zealous servants prayed to God for the salvation of those being served, who were far from the Church fold, is it then believable that such righteous kindled servants, after leaving their physical bodies, would cease praying and supplicating for those whom they loved and for whom they were so zealous for their salvation? There is no doubt they are concerned about us, and some of them currently live amongst us. This is not restricted to the saints and the martyrs, but is also shared by all the righteous and the saints. They pray for us and offer us awesome services.

The Prayer for the Departed

As a conclusion for tonight's sermon, we can say that the prayer for the departed is very useful to the departed. In our Church we celebrate liturgies and raise oblations for our departed loved ones. We believe that such supplications are useful for the righteously departed ones, for the sake of their lapses and mistakes, just as the Church prays in the Litany for the Departed: "Even if any negligence or heedlessness has overtaken them as men, since they were clothed in flesh and dwelt in this world...O Lord, repose and forgive them." Prayers, normally speaking, can never be useful for a wicked person, or for transferring someone from hellfire to the Heavenly Kingdom.

6

Those Qualified for Heaven and Those Forbidden

Heaven Is Man's Homeland and Mother-Country

Who is he who could enter heaven? Who will be deprived of it? These are very serious and important questions. They are important because they concern all of mankind, and are very serious because they relate to their everlasting destiny. With God's grace, we shall attempt to answer these questions within the framework of our solid faith. Before tackling the subject, we wish to remember and confirm two important points:

Heaven is man's homeland. God has made a home for man on earth, which started as the Old Testament temple, and then became the New Testament Church; more importantly, God has prepared for us a home in heaven. The Lord of glory, Jesus said, "In My Father's house are many mansions; if it were not so, I would have told you. I go to prepare a place for you. And if I go and prepare a place for you, I will come again and receive you to Myself; that where I am, there you may be also" (John 14:2–3). Can you imagine that the place where God will be, we shall be also? Sometimes, man stands in amazement before a beautiful picture of the Lord Jesus which expresses His love, tenderness, compassion, care and kindness, painted exquisitely by some artist. How much more so will the real One be like?! We shall not be standing before a symbolic picture, however magnificent it may be, but rather, we shall be with God Himself. God has made a home for man here on earth, and He has prepared for us a home there in heaven after the world will end and pass away. As Saint Paul the apostle expresses, "God becomes the all in all." There will only be left the heavenly homeland and the Church of the first fruits in heaven! Our Church conveys to her believing children in Her worship what awaits them. In the holy liturgy, after the priest says, "Lift up your hearts" The congregation answers, "They are with the Lord." Then they say, "Holy, holy, holy is the Lord of hosts; the whole earth is full of His glory" (Isaiah 6:3). Is not this the angels' praise mentioned in the book of Revelation (4:8)? Is this not the song with which they praise the One sitting on the throne? Likewise, we also pray in the third hour of the Agpeya, "When we stand in Your holy altar, we are counted as standing in heaven."

God does not reject anyone, neither does He forbid anyone from entering heaven. Contrary to this, God, for the sake of bringing man back to his first position, and in order to bring him back to heaven, has given us His Only Begotten Son, out of His love for us. "For God so loved the world that He gave His only begotten Son, that whosoever believes in Him should not perish but have everlasting life" (John 3:16). When God became man, He loved sinners and sought them out, and He proclaimed saying, "For the Son of Man has come to seek and to save that which was lost" (Luke 19:10). The Lord Jesus gave us an excellent parable showing His love to sinners, and His acceptance to them; this is the parable of the Prodigal son, mentioned by Saint Luke in chapter fifteen of his gospel. Saint Peter, moreover, expresses God's love for sinners saying, "The Lord is not slack concerning His promise, as some count slackness, but is longsuffering toward us, not willing that any should perish but that all should come to repentance" (2 Peter 3:9). This is not surprising, for He is God, "who desires all men to be saved and to come to the knowledge of the truth" (1 Timothy 2:4). The human salvation has cost God ever so much! All this is for the sake of returning man back to heaven—his first homeland.

Obstacles for Entering Heaven

1. Reasons for Being Forbidden

Before speaking in details about those people deprived of heaven, it would be better if we first investigate the reasons for this prohibition from heaven.

Sin in its general meaning is a scorn to the Holy God, who, according to His nature, does not accept or endure any sin. How can sin be scornful to God? Sin is scornful to God because it is reckless and careless of His love. God has loved us in a tremendous way, more than we can ever imagine. "No manner of speech can measure the depth of Your love towards mankind" (The Liturgy of Saint Gregory). God "did not spare His own Son, but delivered Him up for us all" (Romans 8:32). What do you call rejecting Him and His love? God searches for us, and we flee from Him and evade Him. God never ceases to invite us and be compassionate to us, and despite this, we reject Him and give Him our backs. God's love never fails. Our dishonestly never stops His honesty. What can we call this? Is this not being scornful to God?

Sin is trespassing over God (1 John 3:4) because it is breaking His commandment.

Sin is to depart from God's obedience. Christ taught us in this way, "If you love Me, keep My commandments" (John 14:15). Our not keeping His commandments, that is, if we do not live them, means we do not love Him. The result is that man, through sin, becomes an enemy to God. "Do you not know that friendship with the world is enmity with God? Whoever therefore wants to be a friend of the world makes himself an enemy of God" (James 4:4). How then can sinners live with God in heaven? Sin is darkness; do darkness and light meet together? God is the Light, and "He dwells in unapproachable light" (1 Timothy 6:16). There is no partnership of the righteous with sinners, for sinners are Satan's children. "You are of your father the devil, and the desires of your father you want to do" (John 8:44). The Lord Jesus made this clear in the parable of the grain and the weeds, when He said, "the good seeds are the sons of the kingdom; the tares are the sons of the wicked one. The enemy who sowed them is the devil" (Matthew 13:38–39).

Furthermore, sin is disobedience against God. To know to what extent our disobedience is harmful, let us remember the children's disobedience to their parents and the harm and agony this causes parents. Man does not bear that his son disobeys and defies him. Man keeps numbering his favors to his son, and his efforts in raising his son, and in enduring hardship so as to make him happy. What can we say about God whom we disobey? We are only a handful of dust from the earth, and despite this, He prolongs His patience and tolerates us!

Rejecting the Entrance through the narrow gate. If sin, in all its aspects, represents the harmful positive side in man's life, then it forms a basic obstruction in entering heaven, causing him to be rejected from entering through the narrow gate. This demonstrates the negative aspect that gradually leads to sin in its absolute positivity. Christ taught us in His teaching the principle of "the narrow gate." In His famous Sermon on the Mount that compiles the basic Christian principles, He said, "Enter by the narrow gate; for wide is the gate and broad is the way that leads to destruction, and there are many who go in by it. Because narrow is the gate and difficult is the way which leads to life, and there are a few who find it" (Matthew 7:13–14). Once, someone came up to the Lord Jesus and asked Him, "Lord, are there few who are saved?" He said to the, "Strive to enter through the narrow gate, for many I say to you, will seek to enter and will not be able" (Luke 13:23–24). Let us meditate on these words, for they imply the answer to the question that concerns the soul's salvation. Christ, here draws the positive correct means for it.

The words "the narrow door" express the behavior of life in a general way. Despite the clear teaching of the Lord Jesus, we find many who rush toward the wide door. It is as if they are saying, "Why do we make things hard for ourselves by fasting for a long time, and by praying the Agpeya, and by the long prayers in Church and by reading the Holy Book and the Psalms? Why do we have this conservative attitude in our attire, with the pretext of being decent? Why do we not just go along with the world and become in their semblance? Why are you making everything so hard for us?" Such ideas are surely behind people's departure from the Churches and from Christ! There is no doubt these words are of Satan's inspiration.

Our saintly fathers held on to this teaching and have carried out this commandment of the Lord's very well. They used to distance themselves from all that is comfortable. They sought all that was hard and wearisome. They were thoroughly convinced they had to walk in the way of Golgotha, toward the cross, in the hope of being blessed with the resurrection joy to come. Those who sow in tears, harvest joyfully.

There is one point that we wish to draw your attention to, before tackling tonight's subject. In addition to the adversary's positive efforts in making people fall into the direct sins, he also finds skillful ways in human deceit. He skillfully uses the system of being hidden. He attempts to convince people there is nothing called Satan! He goes on in his deceits and tells people, "Do not ever believe that you will not enter heaven, for God is very forgiving. His mercy has to extend and include everyone; all will enter heaven. Do you ever think Christ's bloodshed for human salvation could ever be in vain? Never! You will enter heaven." We then answer, "That God is merciful, this is true." Yet, this is not absolutely true. Just as God is merciful, He is also just. Just as He is perfect in His mercy, likewise He is perfect in His justice. We believe we are now on earth in the age of mercy. The repentance door is constantly open before us when we are alive in the body. We can be perfectly blessed with God's mercy. In heaven, after we die, the age of justice begins. In heaven, there is no mercy, because there is no mercy in the judgment to him who has not used mercy in his life. He who says anything different, follows the adversary's concept which is an incorrect concept. The adversary, by doing so, wishes to rob us. Therefore, do not hold on to a half-truth, for mercy and justice are both together in Christ, as it is said in the Psalms, "Mercy and truth have met together; righteousness and peace have kissed each other" (84:10).

2. The Categories of the Forbidden Ones

We cannot explain each of those categories individually for this will be too elaborate. Let us contemplate on some verses mentioned in the Holy Book, where there is reference to some samples of those forbidden to enter heaven:

Saint Paul the apostle mentions some of the forbidden

categories, when he says, "Do you not know that the unrighteous will not inherit the kingdom of God? Do not be deceived. Neither fornicators, nor idolaters, nor adulterers, nor homosexuals, nor sodomites, nor thieves, nor covetous, nor drunkards, nor revilers, nor extortioners will inherit the kingdom of God" (1 Corinthians 6:9–10).

Do you not agree with me that each of these categories needs a long time of meditation and explanation? We will try to be brief in this explanation.

Injustice is unacceptable from the wrongdoer. Even the Church, in the absolution prayer prayed by the priest after the Midnight Prayer, devotes a special part for this, and says, "Lord judge for those who are wronged." We, therefore, pray for the sake of the unjustly treated so that God uplifts the injustice afflicting them. As for those unjust people, they will not inherit the heavenly kingdom. I think there is no dispute about the rest of the forbidden categories, such as the adulterers, the idolaters, the fornicators and the rest of the forbidden list.

Let us stop for a short while at "the ones who insult or curse." Can you imagine that each one who insults another person will not enter the heavenly kingdom? Do not take lightly the cursing sin, for it is equal to the rest of the sins that prevent one from entering heaven!

Saint Paul the apostle mentions another list of the forbidden ones from entering the heavenly kingdom. "But fornication and all uncleanness or covetousness, let it not even be named among you, as is fitting for saints; neither filthiness, nor foolish talking, nor coarse jesting, which are not fitting, but rather giving of thanks. For this you know, that no fornicator, unclean person, nor covetous man, who is an idolater, has any inheritance in the kingdom of Christ and God" (Ephesians 5:3–5).

In the epistle to the Galatians, Saint Paul sets a third list: "Now the works of the flesh are evident, which are: adultery, fornication, uncleanness, lewdness, idolatry, sorcery, hatred, contentions, jealousies, outbursts of wrath, selfish ambitions, dissensions, heresies, envy, murders, drunkenness, revelries, and the like; of which I tell you beforehand, just as I also told you in time past, that those who practice such things will not inherit the kingdom of God" (Galatians 5:19-21). Contemplate with me on these forbidden lists and think of how negligent we are in knowing the divine truth.

There is also a brief comment on the word "factions"; are not the floods of different sects and variable cults in the range of the Christian faith, an ugly form of "factions"? Every faction or crack in the mother Church is the faction that divides the Church in the name of religion; yet religion has nothing to do with it. By means of these things, many lose heaven. What was said by the apostle is the most eloquent proof, "Anger, quarrels, dissensions, factions." It is a chain of those ones forbidden from entering heaven! If we meditate on the book of Revelation, the book that speaks to us of heaven, life-after and judgment, we will find Saint John recording to us an atrocious list of those forbidden. He says, "But the cowardly, unbelieving, abominable, murderers, sexually immoral, sorcerers, idolaters, and all liars shall have their part in the lake which burns with fire and brimstone, which is the second death" (21:8).

If we meditate on this list, we shall see that on top

of the list are the cowardly and the unbelievers. Those who fear are like the unbelievers who will perish. We also find in this list "all liars." Whatever motive there may be behind lying and however much some try to call lying something else, like "a white lie," yet all of those who will lie will perish.

After this quick survey of the list of those forbidden from heaven, let us choose some of those forbidden ones, and try to shed some more light on them:

a. *Pride.* This is the foremost sin that prevents man from heaven. Was not Satan an archangel, and yet he fell due to his pride? Thus, he tries to make man fall in the same sin of pride and arrogance. When Satan went into the serpent, and when he began to speak to Eve, he came forth with a scornful question, "Has God truly said, 'Eat not of every tree of the garden?'" (Genesis 3:1). When the woman replied, "We may eat of the fruits of the trees of the garden, but of the fruit of the tree which is in the midst of the garden, God said, 'You shall not eat of it, neither shall you touch it, lest you die'" (Genesis 3:3). At this point, Satan intervened and said, "You shall not surely die! For God knew that in whatever day you should eat of it , your eyes would be opened, and you would be as gods, knowing good and evil" (Genesis 3:5).

You will not die, for you will become gods...this is pride! Therefore, the human downfall was due to the sin of arrogance. Arrogance, or pride, is one of the mother sins from which branches out many other sins; so we have to be constantly careful of falling into the sin of pride. The apostle said, "God resists the proud, but gives grace to the humble" (James 4:6). Meditate on the deep meaning behind these words: "God resists the proud." Although God hates all sins and He hates all evil, there is no sin mentioned in the Holy Book in such a way. We have not read in the Holy Book, from its beginning to its end, that God resists a particular sin except that of pride. God resists the proud...He not only hates the sin of pride, but He resists it as well.

Long ago, the sin of pride belonged to the scribes and the Pharisees. The Lord Jesus summarized it by saying about them, "For they loved the praise of men more than the praise of God" (John 12:43).

Christ forgave the adulteress who was brought forth to Him and was caught red-handed. He therefore said to her, "Neither do I condemn you; go and sin no more" (John 8:3–11). Whereas Christ blamed the scribes and the Pharisees with so many "woes," for they were hypocrites and arrogant people who loved the foremost seats and the people's praise and their flattering words (Matthew 23).

I fear some of us may say, "Thank God, we are not arrogant, we have gotten rid of this primary sin." I also fear some may think that to not be proud, a man needs to say about himself that he is a sinner and miserable and that he does not understand. He might pretend to be modest and bend his head down to the ground, and speak softly and humble himself in the tone of his voice, while thinking that these affectations are qualities of humility! The issue of pride and modesty are much deeper than that. The range of measurement for pride and humility is man's thoughts and his heart. The real humility is that man knows himself well, and his inner self in truth. Let man understand he is only a handful of the earth's dust that is trodden down by man's feet. Because of this, Saint Augustine used to cry out to God, saying, "O my God, let me know who I am, and who You are." If only man knew himself well, he would be relieved of so many sins.

b. Lack of Faith. One of the basic and foremost facts that prevent man from entering heaven is his lack of faith. We have seen in Revelation 21:8 that the cowardly and the unbelievers have come on top of the list of the forbidden ones to go to heaven. There is great concord between fear and the lack of faith; for how can fear cannot agree with faith? Let us meditate on the Psalms 23 and 27, both written by David the Prophet: "The Lord is my shepherd, I shall not want...Yea, though I walk in the midst of the shadow of death, I shall fear no evil; for You are with me." And "The Lord is my light and my Savior; whom shall I fear? The Lord is the defender of my life; of whom shall I be afraid? When evildoers drew near against me to eat up my flesh, my persecutors and my enemies, they fainted and fell. Though an army should set itself in array against me, my heart shall not be afraid; Though war should rise up against me, in this am I confident." How awesome these words are! Indeed, fear is an enemy of the faith. This is why we cannot say that a coward is a believer; and lest some become burdened with these words, we wish to make this matter clear, so they feel emotionally at peace. There is not doubt that fear is a normal instinct in man, for fear is one of our inherent instincts. Some are afraid of the dark, others are afraid of dogs. Also, women and girls have a more susceptible heart than men, and so we find the phenomenon of fear to be more obvious with them. This does not mean that men do not get afraid, for they surely fear a lot of things. Despite these examples that show the normal fear, we can assure you that if there is strong faith, then fear vanishes. Anyone who feels and believes God is with him will not fear, because, "if God is for us, who can be against us?" (Romans 8:31).

All unrighteousness grows, just as faith, humility and love grow. About this growth, Saint Paul the apostle says, "till we all come to the unity of the faith and of the knowledge of the Son of God, to a perfect man, to the measure of the stature of the fullness of Christ" (Ephesians 4:13). It is important we grow in virtues and righteousness and be exalted in them, until Christ becomes the prime among many brethren. If anyone is struck with fear, he has to immediately treat it with faith. But we have to be cautious not to exaggerate this fear lest it lead us to assume we shall not go to heaven. Such a feeling of despair is a big sin. If we possess the true faith, our fears will be scattered, whatever they may be. The sin of "lack of faith" mentioned by Saint John in Revelation 2:18, surely means "the lack of Christian faith," and the lack of faith in the salvation which Christ has fulfilled.

What is amazing is that some think the good people of the unbelievers could be blessed with the heavenly glory. But this assumption is wrong. The Lord's words to Nicodemus concerning this issue are clear indeed: "He who believes in Him is not condemned; but he who does not believe is condemned already, because he has not believed in the name of the only begotten Son of God.

And this is the condemnation, that the light has come into the world, and men loved darkness rather than light, because their deeds were evil" (John 3:18–19). There is no doubt, therefore, that unbelievers will not enter heaven and that Christ's blood shed on the cross will not be wasted in vain!

What is man's punishment when he rejects Christ's salvation? Saint Paul the apostle answers this question saying, "How shall we escape if we neglect so great a salvation, which at the first began to be spoken by the Lord, and was confirmed to us by those who heard Him" (Hebrews 2:3). Yes, how can we escape if we neglect so great a salvation? There is no rescue for that!

As for the believers who are as such by name only: these men have a greater sin, because he who knows more is asked to do more (Luke 12:48). As the Lord Jesus said, "If you were blind, you would have no sin; but now you say, 'We see.' Therefore your sin remains" (John 9:41).

Dear brethren, I wish we were more conscious of ourselves. How many liturgies do we attend and how much preaching do we hear and how many books do we read? How many times do we partake of the Lord's Holy Body and His blood? Despite all this, where did our life reach? After all of this spiritual food, we hope we have drawn closer to heaven, as Saint Paul the apostle says, "For our citizenship is in heaven" (Philippians 3:20). If we live, right now, physically on earth, then our life is supposed to be up in heaven. How often did we hear the words said by the Lord Jesus Christ about Jerusalem, "O Jerusalem, Jerusalem, the one who kills the prophets and stones those who are sent to her! How often I wanted to gather your children together, as a hen gathers her chicks under her wings, but you were not willing! See! Your house is left to you desolate" (Matthew 23:37–38). The words "how often," and "you were not willing... your house is left to you desolate," these same words are addressed by Jesus to us: "How often have I desired... and you were not willing!" The prophet warns us, "Therefore, as the Holy Spirit says: 'Today, if you will hear His voice, Do not harden your hearts as in the rebellion" (Hebrews 3:7–8). This is God's voice. This voice reverberates in the Church sides, and if you hear God's voice, do not harden your hearts. Faith that is apparent and only in words is of no use, for the heart is very far away. This is why Saint James the apostle says, "But someone will say, 'You have faith, and I have works.' Show me your faith without your works, and I will show you my faith by my works. You believe that there is one God. You do well. Even the demons believe—and tremble! But do you want to know, O foolish man, that faith without works is dead" (2:18–20).

Christianity does not ask the believer merely to reiterate phrases that have the meaning of faith, but Christianity asks that with faith, there should be works. Therefore, we find the American proverb that says, "Actions speak louder than words." That is, the works are much more important than mere words. I wish we make our deeds speak of our true Christian faith.

c. Hypocrisy. This is one more category that will not enter heaven—the category of the hypocrites. Some may say this category goes under the motto of the sin of arrogance. Some others may say it is a category that enters in the apparent and seeming faith. I preferred to devote a special place so that we shed more light on it. The Lord Jesus, to Him be the glory, said in His sermon on the mount, "Many will say to Me in that day, 'Lord, Lord have we not...cast out demons in Your name, and done many wonders in Your name?' And then I will declare to them, 'I never knew you, depart from Me, you who practice lawlessness'" (Matthew 7:22–23). The phrase, 'I never knew you' means that the Lord Jesus did not know these people before. In this way, the entering into heaven and getting prepared for it begins here on earth. If the university student in not allowed to sit for the exam unless he fulfills a percentage of the designated lecture attendance for every subject, accordingly no one will enter heaven unless he fulfills an attendance percentage in the different spiritual subjects, whether in prayer, in abstinence, in Christian virtues, etc.

Here on earth, you can decide if it is your right to enter heaven or not. But after the termination of our life on earth, it is of no avail, for the door will be shut. This is clear from the parable of the ten virgins in Matthew 25. In this parable there is an awesome expression, "the door was shut"; what a catastrophe! Some will try to knock on the door, pleading and begging, "Lord, Lord, open to us!" (25:1). Then the Divine Voice will come to them, "I do not know you, go away from Me you evil doers!" Every person who wishes to enter the kingdom of heaven has to come to know God our Lord when he/she is here on earth. If the fruit tree planted by man does not give forth delicious fruits except after years of growth, then likewise is the attainment of heaven, which is the priceless and delicious fruit. We have to toil and plant it now, so that we may harvest it after we move there. Whatever man plants, he reaps. Those who sow in tears, harvest joyfully.

d. Adultery. We spoke of this sin in detail in a previous discussion. At this point we shall offer a simplified version of this horrific sin that forbids man from entering heaven. The Christian believer has become, through the unity with Christ, a temple of God and a dwelling place for His Holy Spirit. "Do you not know that you are the temple of God and that the Spirit of God dwells in you? If anyone defiles the temple of God, God will destroy him. For the temple of God is holy, which temple you are" (1 Corinthians 3:16, 17). The Christian believer has become a member in Christ's body that is invisible (Colossians 1:18, 3:15; Ephesians 1:22–23). Saint Paul says, "Do you not know that your bodies are members of Christ? Shall I then take the members of Christ and make them members of a harlot? Certainly not! Or do you not know that he who is joined to a harlot is one body with her? For "the two," He says, "shall become one flesh." But he who is joined to the Lord is one spirit with Him. Flee sexual immorality. Every sin that a man does is outside the body, but he who commits sexual immorality sins against his own body" (1 Corinthians 6:15–18).

e. Hatred and Murder. Saint John the Apostle says, "Whoever hates his brother is a murderer, and you know that no murderer has eternal life abiding in him" (1 John 3:15). We can summarize Christianity and its message into three golden words written in letters of light, "God is love." Christianity does not command love according to the worldly concept, but it commands the love of our enemies and blessing them and praying for their sake. "But I say to you, love your enemies, bless those who curse you, do good to those who hate you, and pray for those who spitefully use you and persecute you, that you may be sons of your Father in heaven; for He makes His sun rise on the evil and on the good, and sends rain on the just and on the unjust" (Matthew 5:44–45). Christianity, by the teaching to love one's enemies and to pray for them, aims at transforming them to loved ones. "Therefore, 'If your enemy is hungry, feed him; If he is thirsty, give him a drink; For in so doing you will heap coals of fire on his head.' Do not be overcome by evil, but overcome evil with good" (Romans 12:20–21). Perfect love is the passport for going into heaven. As for hatred, it is a candid command of being forbidden to enter heaven—the dwelling place of the God of love.

If we are speaking of the hatred that leads to homicide, this can refer to abortion, which is the killing of a soul. We do not wish to dwell on this matter, for we have spoken of it in our study of the sixth commandment of the Ten Commandments on a previous occasion. At this point, we are only reminding you of its importance.

f. Magic and Sorcery. They also are included in the list of those ones forbidden to enter the heavenly kingdom.

Among this group, are all those who exorcise the spirits and the like. The Holy Book is full of verses that denounce this deprived category of heaven. God was careful, since the older times, to warn His people of the magicians, the sorcerers, fortunetellers, and exorcists. He therefore said, "You shall not save the lives of sorcerers" (Exodus 22:18). And also, "And the soul that shall follow those who have in them divining spirits, or enchanters, so as to whore after them; I will set My face against that soul, and will destroy it from among its people...And as for a man or woman whosoever of them shall have in them a divining spirit, or be an enchanter, let them both die the death: you shall stone them with stones, they are guilty" (Leviticus 20:6, 27). After listening to these clear words, is anyone going to be weakened and resort to magicians and sorcerers in Satanic attempts to decipher such things? Let us ask ourselves now, who is the stronger one, God or Satan? If Satan were strong, then let us depart from God and follow Satan. God forbid it should be this way. For God is stronger, in an immeasurable way, than any other power. It is true that God sometimes allows Satan to show his strength, just as He has allowed the Egyptian magicians in the days of Moses to perform things in the same manner as Moses. But as soon as we reach the third strike, we see the inability of the Egyptian magicians to cope with the wonders of Moses. Thus, they admit to Pharaoh their impotence, saying, "This is the finger of God" (Exodus 8:19). Therefore, do not be troubled by any problem and do not resort to Satan, for when the problem chain becomes crucial indeed, the relief is near, coming from God. Therefore, be patient, and still more patient. Patience will not only relieve you of the problem, but it will also lead you to heaven. By your patience, you will possess yourself, and he who is patient to the end will be saved. So be patient, and do not weaken. Relief is at the door, as the poet says, "It has become tight; and when the chain is really difficult, relief comes, whereas I thought it would never come!"

g. Idol Worship. These do not mean those ones who worship statues. The worshipping of idols includes many categories. God said, "And you shall love the Lord your God with all your heart, with all your soul, with all your mind, and with all your strength" (Mark 12:30). This means that the deepest core of man has to be to God, and God alone. Hence, if you worship anyone other than God, then this is the worshipping of idols. Such an example is the following:

Someone who loves a girl to the extent of worshipping her and vice versa. Is this not a kind of idol worshipping? Yes it is indeed! Each of their hearts has become preoccupied with the other, and thus, there is no place in the heart for God. The beloved has therefore been changed to an idol, worshipped by the lover.

The worshipping of the body is another kind of idol worshipping. A woman who is concerned about her body, to the extent of worshipping it: She stands before the mirror for long hours, trying to adorn her body with the best things; She tries to wear and beautify herself by using the best makeup and perfume she could buy; She has nothing to preoccupy herself with other than her own body. The same thing could also happen to a young man.

Is this not a kind of idol worshipping? The body has thus become a mere idol before which we burn the incense.

Money is a tremendous and very serious idol, which many worship and serve. The Lord Jesus said, "No one can serve two masters; for either he will hate the one and love the other, or else he will be loyal to the one and despise the other. You cannot serve God and mammon" (Matthew 6:24). Anyone who loves money cannot love God. Some attempt to deceive themselves and say that they pay the tithe offerings to God, and so there is nothing more to give to God. But this is self-deception. "But whoever has this world's goods, and sees his brother in need, and shuts up his heart from him, how does the love of God abide in Him? My little children, let us not love in word or in tongue, but in deed and in truth" (1 John 3:17–18). Let us not put to sleep our conscience by assuming that just paying the tithes is enough to put responsibility aside from us. The Lord of Glory has taught us that he desires mercy and not sacrifice. God does not care about your money; He rather cares more about your heart.

If you happen to meet someone in need, you have to be merciful toward him, and you have to try to save him from his problems. Mediate well on the Acts of the Apostles Chapter 4 to know how the first church dealt with money, and how the well-to-do believers used to sell their property and possessions and put the money under the feet of the apostles. The real place for money in Christ's church is at the feet of the Apostles. Money is under the feet of God's men, but he who puts money on top of him is enslaved to it and is dominated by it. It is true that money is a gift from God, but He gave us the money so we use it, not that the money uses us.

One of the most impressive examples of those enslaved by money is the story of the rich young man who came to the Lord Jesus Christ in eagerness, and asked what he could do to inherit eternal life. When Christ replied, "You know the commandments...He answered and said to Him, 'Teacher, all these things I have kept from my youth.' Then Jesus, looking at him, loved him, and said to him, 'One thing you lack: Go your way, sell whatever you have and give to the poor, and you will have treasure in heaven; and come, take up the cross, and follow Me.' But he was sad at this word, and went away sorrowful, for he had great possessions"(Mark 10:19–22). What a pity for this young man: a little while ago, he was eager to know the way to the heavenly kingdom. Though Christ loved him, yet the young man would not be able to get rid of the love of money. He, therefore, left Christ and left the way to eternal life, and went away sorrowfully because he loved his money more than he loved God. Hence, money is a dangerous idol. There are so many people who leave God in order to worship money. Saint Paul the Apostle said a most impressive quote about the worshipping of money, "For the love of money is a root of all kinds of evil, for which some have strayed from the faith in their greediness, and pierced themselves through with many sorrows" (1 Timothy 6:10). This is the money that forms a drastic obstruction that prevents many from entering the heavenly kingdom!

h. Liars. One of the categories forbidden from entering

heaven, as mentioned in the list is the book of Revelation, are liars. The liar, my brethren, is forbidden to enter the kingdom of heaven. The first lie in human history is that of Satan's lie to Eve. He lied to her when he told her, "You shall not surely die" (Genesis 3:5). The second lie was Cain's lie after killing his brother Abel. When God asked him where Abel his brother was, he lied to God, and said, "Am I my brother's keeper?" (Genesis 4:9). Therefore, lying is an abhorred sin. It often happens that lying comes as a second sin. What does a second sin mean?

It means that man commits a certain sin and afterwards he lies in order to cover up the first sin. But as we know the cord for lying is a short one. If lying is able to save someone for a moment, it is surely unable to save him to the end, for soon enough his lying is revealed. This truth has been declared openly by our Lord Jesus Christ, to Him be the glory, when he said, "For nothing is secret that will not be revealed, nor anything hidden that will not be known and come to light" (Luke 8:17). Therefore, everything will be revealed and proclaimed before all people, and we shall be the laughing stock before everyone.

In addition to all this, God's wrath will befall us, and we shall lose our exalted gain in heaven! Every liar is considered by the Lord Jesus to be a son of Satan. "You are of your father the devil, and the desires of your father you want to do. He was a murderer from the beginning, and does not stand in the truth, because there is no truth in him. When he speaks a lie, he speaks from his own resources, for he is a liar and the father of it" (John 8:44). Therefore, Satan is the father of every liar.

To speak about those forbidden from entering heaven

is as speaking about those qualified for going into the heavenly kingdom. For when we have spoken about what is contrary to those sins, we also indicate the opposite may lead to entering the kingdom of heaven.

The Qualifications for Entering Heaven

It is profitable indeed for everyone to consider carefully those well-equipped for heaven, so that he attempts to be one of them. We have to be sure of the basic facts, that the foremost qualification for heaven is not the personal virtue, but rather the faith in Christ's salvation and the second birth.

1. The Faith in Christ's Salvation

This is the foremost qualification for heaven, but it is not a personal qualification. We have obtained this salvation for free, without any favor on our part. No man will be able to enter heaven without having the absolute faith in the salvation fulfilled by Christ. It is not a theoretical faith, rather, it is practical and actual faith. As Saint James the Apostle says, "even the demons believe—and tremble!" (2:19).

A great deal has been said of Christ's salvation. Actually, it is the focus of the entire Holy Book and its aim. There is no other aim except this one in its importance. It is wonderful indeed what Saint Peter the Apostle said of Christ, "Nor is there salvation in any other, for there is no other name under heaven given among men by which we must be saved" (Acts 4:12). Let us meditate for long on the meaning of this verse "Nor is there salvation in any other." There is no one other than Christ in whom there is salvation, and there will be no one else. Wretched indeed are those people who do not understand this gleaming truth. Saint Thomas the Apostle asked the Lord Jesus, "How can we know the way?" The Lord's answer for his question was as clear as could possible be, "I am the way, the truth, and the life. No one comes to the Father except through Me" (John 14:5–6). The way is Christ, and there is no salvation by anyone else. He also said about Himself, "I am the door. If anyone enters by Me, he will be saved, and will go in and out and find pasture" (John 10:9). The door is the entrance, and he who does not enter by the door, will be kept out! Moreover, he who "climbs up some other way, the same is a thief and a robber" (John 10:1). Also, "He who believes in the Son has everlasting life; and he who does not believe the Son shall not see life, but the wrath of God abides on him" (John 3:36).

Dear brethren, I wish we understand religion not as a mere urge for righteousness and a prohibition for unrighteousness. This is a Satanic deceit. Even if every religion urges righteousness and prohibits evil and vice, yet in Christianity, religion is something other than that. The old creation that has fallen and consequently been corrupted, can never enter heaven. The corruptible can never inherit the incorruptible. Man has to be renewed so he becomes a new creation. This is fulfilled by Christ and in Christ. Why should it be Christ? Saint Paul answers, saying, "Therefore He is also able to save to the uttermost those who come to God through Him, since He always lives to make intercession for them" (Hebrews 7:25). Let us remember the words of the Lord Jesus that Saint John recorded in his holy gospel, "Whatever you ask in My name, that I will do, that the Father may be glorified in the Son. If you ask anything in My name, I will do it" (John 14:13–14). "Most assuredly, I say to you, whatever you ask the Father in My name He will give you. Until now you have asked nothing in My name. Ask, and you will receive, that your joy may be full" (John 16:23–24).

Here we find the answer to the question some people ask as to why the church has added the phrase "in Christ Jesus our Lord" to the Lord's prayer. It is because without Christ we are of no value whatsoever. We do not have any acceptance from God. For I, without Christ, am worth nothing at all and have nothing to do with the Father. Rather, without Him, I am a sinful and guilty person. With faith in Christ's salvation, I have the rights to His blood that was shed on the cross and the wonderful redemption He paid instead of me, for me and for the entire world. I have a great privilege, that I have become God's son and an heir with Christ in all the heavenly glory!

Pray, my brethren, so that the Lord reveals Himself to those who do not know Him. Pray for the salvation of the world. "He who believes in Him is not condemned; but he who does not believe is condemned already, because he has not believed in the name of the only begotten Son of God. And this is the condemnation, that the light has come into the world, and men loved darkness rather than light, because their deeds were evil" (John 3:18–19).

Saint John speaks of heaven and says, "But there shall by no means enter it anything that defiles, or causes an abomination or a lie, but only those who are written in the Lamb's Book of Life" (Revelation 21:27). Who is this Lamb? He is the slaughtered Lamb...He is the Christ who was slaughtered for us as a Passover, by which He redeemed us. Everything in heaven is related to the slaughtered Lamb. Anyone whose name is not written in the Lamb's Book of Life will not be destined for salvation, and thus he will perish. He has nothing ahead of him except the terrifying judgment.

2. The Second Birth

This is the second prerequisite for entering heaven. The second birth is what we call the baptism.

I desire you open your hearts, minds and ears to the following.

There are two worlds: the natural world, which is the material world around us, and the world of the spirit, which is heaven. For man to enter the world of nature, that is this world, he has to be born of a father and a mother. Likewise with the world of the spirit, that is, heaven; one has to be born spiritually from God and the church. In this way, God will become his Father, and the Church will become his Mother. He who is not born twice will not enter heaven. The first birth is the physical one from the father and mother. The second birth is from God and the Church, by means of the holy baptism. By the first birth he enters the natural world, and by the second birth he enters heaven. Without the first birth he will not see the earth, and without the second birth he will not witness heaven. There is no other alternative. This issue is as clear as could be in Christ's discussion with Nicodemus, the Jewish teacher, "Most assuredly, I say to you, unless one is born again, he cannot see the kingdom of God." When Nicodemus asked in amusement, "How can a man be born when he is old? Can he enter a second time into his mother's womb and be born?" Christ's answer to him was, "Most assuredly, I say to you, unless one is born of water and the Spirit, he cannot enter the kingdom of God. That which is born of the flesh is flesh, and that which is born of the Spirit, is spirit. Do not marvel that I said to you, 'You must be born again'" (John 3:1–7). Let us meditate on the words Christ said, "He cannot enter the kingdom of God" even if he wants, he is unable to.

3. Christian Virtues

After the first two major prerequisites, the Christian virtues, which are the fruits of the Holy Spirit in us. "For the fruit of the Spirit is in all goodness, righteousness, and truth" (Ephesians 5:9). A person who has none of these virtues, to him apply the words of the Baptist, "even now the ax is laid to the root of the trees. Therefore every tree which does not bear good fruit is cut down and thrown into the fire" (Matthew 3:10). Concerning this tree that does not give forth fruit, the Lord Jesus, to Him be the glory, has said, "Cut it down, why does it use up the ground?" (Luke 13:7).

We are actually in need of time if we wish to possess all the virtues by words. The saintly fathers have called them, "the mother virtues." These are the virtues that give birth to other virtues, such as faith, hope and love, as mentioned by Saint Paul. Also, the pure in heart, shall see God (Matthew 5:8). Moreover, modesty comes on top of the list for virtues. Christ began His sermon on the mount by blessing the meek in the Spirit and said that theirs is the kingdom of heaven. Spiritual meekness, as our fathers the saints have taught us, is the essential foundation for all the other virtues.

In conclusion, those qualified to enter heaven have to be saints according to the words of our teacher Saint Paul, "the holiness, without which no one will see the Lord" (Hebrews 12:14). "Just as He chose us in Him before the foundation of the world, that we should be holy and without blame before Him" (Ephesians 1:4). "But as He who called you is holy, you also be holy in all your conduct, because it is written, 'Be holy, for I am holy'" (1 Peter 1:15–16). God, who is holy, cannot be seen except by those who are holy. We think it enough on this issue, because if we with to discuss elaborately all what those qualified for heaven should be adorned with, we would need the time and the lectures to do so.

7

The End of the World and Christ's Second Coming

This is a topic that preoccupies all of us, because there is no one who disregards the end of the world and the second advent of our Lord Jesus. He will come suddenly to judge the world. It will not be the same as it is now. If the Lord has been patient enough with us and has showed us His tenderness and His compassion, the situation will not be the same in the time of judgment.

It is enough to put before our eyes this terrifying picture, drawn for us in the book of Revelation about what will happen on this awesome and horrifying day: "And the kings of the earth, the great men, the rich men, the commanders, the mighty men, every slave and every free man, hid themselves in the caves and in the rocks of the mountains, and said to the mountains and rocks, 'Fall on us and hide us from the face of Him who sits on the throne and from the wrath of the Lamb! For the great day of His wrath has come, and who is able to stand?'" (6:15–16).

Let us all know that we are now in the beginning of the end, for we are not of darkness, but all of us are sons of light and day. The Lord has given us these signs so that this day will not surprise. We should be aware and cautious, and correct our conduct immediately, as well as our deeds and our thoughts. Christ, to Him be the glory, has two advents: the first advent was in the fullness of time, when He was born of the Holy Spirit and of the pure Virgin, the chaste Mother of Light, Saint Mary.

In this advent, He was manifested in the flesh to be witnessed by everyone, so as to complete salvation for the entire world, when He was hung on the cross. He died and rose from the dead and ascended into the heavens. As for His Second Coming, about which we are speaking now, this is His advent for judgment; for Christ is the Judge Who will judge the entire world. He Himself says with His blessed, divine mouth, "For the Father judges no one, but has committed all judgment to the Son" (John 5:22).

Christ's Second Coming Is an Assured Fact

Christ's Second Coming is an assured fact that cannot be argued about, and is not controversial in any way. It is one of the major Christian facts, and is the creed of all the sects and the various Christian trends. This is the result of the clear manifestations so obviously mentioned in the Holy Gospel, primarily spoken of by the words of

Christ Himself.

The Lord Jesus says, "Then the sign of the Son of Man will appear in heaven, and then all the tribes of the earth will mourn, and they will see the Son of Man coming on the clouds of heaven with power and great glory" (Matthew 24:30). "When the Son of Man comes in His glory, and all the holy angels with Him, then He will sit on the throne of His glory" (Matthew 25:31). "And then they will see the Son of Man coming in a cloud with power and great glory" (Luke 21:27).

As for Saint Paul the Apostle, he repeats this fact quite often: "eagerly waiting for the revelation of our Lord Jesus' Christ" (1 Corinthians 1:7). Here, the "revelation" means the appearance of the Lord. "Therefore, judge nothing before the time, until the Lord comes, who will both bring to light the hidden things of darkness and reveal the counsels of the heart" (1 Corinthians 4:5). "But each one in his own order: Christ the firstfruits, afterward those who are Christ's at his coming" (1 Corinthians 15:23). "For our citizenship is in heaven, from which we also eagerly wait for the Savior, the Lord Jesus Christ" (Philippians 3:20). "When Christ who is our life appears, then you also will appear with Him in glory" (Colossians 3:4). "And to wait for His Son from heaven, whom He raised from the dead, even Jesus who delivers us from the wrath to come" (1 Thessalonians 1:10). "For the Lord Himself will descend from heaven with a shout, with the voice of an archangel, and with the trumpet of God" (1 Thessalonians 4:16). Saint Paul the Apostle commands his disciple Timothy, saying, "I urge you...to keep this commandment without spot, blameless until our Lord

Jesus Christ's appearing" (1 Timothy 6:14). "Looking for the blessed hope and glorious appearing of our great God and Savior Jesus Christ" (Titans 2:13). In his epistle to the Hebrews, he says, "So Christ was offered once to bear the sins of many. To those who eagerly wait for Him He will appear a second time, apart from sin, for salvation" (Hebrews 9:28).

As for Saint Peter the Apostle, he says, "Looking for and hastening the coming of the day of God" (2 Peter 3:12).

Saint John the Apostle confirms the Lord's Second Coming, "but we know that when He is revealed, we shall be like Him, for we shall see Him as He is" (1 John 3:2). These are just a few of the many testimonies in the blessed gospel that show us clearly Christ's Second Coming. From these testimonies, it is clear that Christ, to Him be the glory, will not only come, but He will also come and be seen by everyone as the angels have said to the disciples after His holy ascension, "Men of Galilee, why do you stand gazing up into heaven? This same Jesus, who was taken up from you into heaven, will so come in like manner as you saw Him go into heaven" (Acts 1:11). Moreover, Saint John says in the book of Revelation when speaking of the Lord of glory, "Behold, He is coming with clouds, and every eye will see Him, even they who pierced Him. And all the tribes of the earth will mourn because of Him" (1:7).

The Time of the Second Coming

We have seen a general agreement about Christ's Second Coming. Many have fallen into the mistake of attempting to specify the time of this advent. Defining a specific time for Christ's coming is not correct, for many reasons:

It contradicts the text of the Holy Gospel. The Lord Jesus has said, "But of that day and hour no one knows, not even the angels of heaven, but My Father only... Watch, therefore, for you do not know what hour your Lord is coming.... Therefore you also be ready, for the Son of Man is coming at an hour you do not expect" (Matthew 24:36, 42, 44). When Christ was assembled with His disciples directly before His ascension, they asked Him a question related to this issue, and His answer was, "It is not for you to know times or seasons which the Father has put in His own authority" (Acts 1:7). Furthermore, the Lord Jesus declares this coming will be all of a sudden, as the lightning is. "For as the lightning comes from the east and flashes to the west, so also will the coming of the Son of Man be" (Matthew 24:27). Lightening is quick and sudden. A sudden matter cannot be previously announced, otherwise this suddenness is cancelled. Therefore, specifying Christ's time for His Second Coming is incorrect, and it contradicts the written testimonial texts.

Specifying the time of Christ's Second Coming is not in accordance with God's will in hiding this day and this hour from being known. As for God's will in doing so, it is to make all the people in a state of constant preparation. We can compare this to a teacher who tries to urge his students to study their lessons constantly, telling them he would test them anytime, with no set time for the test. This is the same intention of Christ, who said, after He had spoken of the signs pertaining to the end of the world, and the end of times, "Take heed, watch and pray; for you do not know when the time is" (Mark 13:33). For a similar purpose, Christ hid from man the time of his death, so he would be constantly prepared to meet the Lord. If man knew the time of his departure from this world and that he still has many years to live, this would be a motivation for him to be negligent and delay his repentance for some other time. Furthermore, the opportunity could slip away from him.

Specifying the time for Christ's Second Coming and the extinction of this world, contradicts God's wisdom in making people spend their life in activity and without any negligence. The Christian's feeling that the world will pass away and that the Lord will come could lead him to cease all his work in the expectation of this hour. This could also make people become careless and the process of work action would come to a stop in every field of life. Some Christians in the Apostles' time fell into this mistake, which made Saint Paul intervene to correct this erroneous concept. Therefore he wrote to the Thessalonians saying, "Now concerning the coming of our Lord Jesus Christ, and our assembling to meet Him, we beg you, brethren, not to be quickly shaken in mind or excited, either by spirit or by word, or by letter purporting to be from us, to the effect that the day of the Lord has come. Let no one deceive you in any way...Do you remember that when I was still with you I told you this?" (2 Thessalonians 2:1–5). Some Christian sects have deviated and dared enough to specify the time of Christ's coming, mentioning the year, the day and the hour. This time has passed, of course, without the coming of Christ. This was shameful indeed, and their lies were exposed to everyone. This conduct is absolutely wrong, and its impact harms Christianity to the greatest extent; in addition to the impact of these prophecies, many Christians fell into carelessness and many non-Christians make fun of such a matter.

Signs That Precede the Second Coming

Though Christ hid the exact time of His Second Coming, due to His wisdom, yet He gave the signs that point to the closeness of His coming. Before going into this topic, we wish to notify you that the passages dealing with the end of the world and Christ's Second Coming in the Holy Gospels, specifically Saint Matthew 24, Saint Mark 13 and Saint Luke 21.

We notice there is the link between the words about the end of the world and that of the destruction of Jerusalem and its temple. This is none other than the destruction of Jerusalem and its temple, with all the ordeals and hardships implied. This is only a miniature picture of what would happen at the end of the world, prior to Christ's Second Coming. So what are the signs that precede Christ's Second Coming?

1. The Persecution of the Believers

This is the foremost sign mentioned by the Lord Jesus, to Him be the glory. "But before all these things, they will lay their hands on you and persecute you, delivering you up to the synagogues and prisons. You will be brought before kings and rulers for My name's sake" (Luke 21:12).

The church history since its establishment and its appearance on the historical stage assures the truth of this. The Christians were faced with animosity even from the closest ones to them, which proves that the Lord Jesus , to Him be the glory, was correct when He said, "You will be betrayed even by parents and brothers, relatives and friends; and they will put some of you to death" (Luke 21:16).

We should not be scared or panic from this sign. If Christ has given us this sign in advance, yet He gave us, together with it, precious promises indeed: that He will be with us all the days until the end of times (Matthew 28:20); that the door of Hades will not prevail over the church. His care is so awesome that He said not one of the hairs on our head would perish. Throughout all of this, we need to be patient (Luke 21:18–19).

Our forefathers and ancestors have paid a tremendous price for this faith, their life. Today, we do not pay such a price! God, due to His awesome love, knows the weakness of our love now, and thus He does not permit us to be tempted more than we can endure. Despite this, some regress from the faith and their self-will weakens and diminishes. These lose their faith out of their own self-will, because they do not know the value of this faith! They are similar to a child who leaves very easily some gold jewelry or a precious pen in exchange for a piece of candy. This is only because he does not know the value of what he had and does not benefit from it, and moreover, he does not know how to use it.

Because our ancestors knew the value of their faith in Christ, they were firm in it until the very end. They preferred to give up their life rather than lose their most holy faith. They believed the shame of Christ richer than all the treasures of the world. This is similar to what was said of Moses, "By faith, Moses, when he became of age, refused to be called the son of Pharaoh's daughter, choosing rather to suffer affliction with the people of God than to enjoy the passing pleasures of sin, esteeming the reproach of Christ greater riches than the treasures in Egypt; for he looked to the reward" (Hebrews 11:24–26).

2. The Appearance of the Prophets and the False Christs

This is the second sign for the Second Coming, made clear to us by the Lord Jesus, to Him be the glory, when He said, "False christs and false prophets will rise and show signs and wonders to deceive, if possible, even the elect" (Mark 13:22). Also, "Many will come in My name, saying, 'I am He,' And will deceive many" (Mark 13:6). This prophecy has partially been fulfilled, for many false christs and false prophets have appeared since the dawn of Christianity.

Some are mentioned in the New Testament and some are recorded in history.

Among these are Bar-Jesus who our teachers Saint Paul the Apostle met in Paphos in the island of Cyprus. He tried to obstruct the message of Saint Paul the Apostle concerning faith in the island and to Sergius the proconsul. Therefore, the Lord struck him with blindness (Acts 13:6–12). We also read about Simon the magician who amazed the people of Samaria with his magic. Thus they followed him from the eldest to the youngest and said that he was God's great strength. The two apostles Saint Peter and Saint John met him in Samaria. When he saw the wonders they did, he asked them to give him the grace of priesthood. Saint Peter said to him, "You have neither part nor portion in this matter, for your heart is not right in the sight of God. Repent therefore of this your wickedness, and pray God if perhaps the thought of your heart may be forgiven you. For I see that you are poisoned by bitterness and bound by iniquity" (Acts 8:21–23).

There are many other references to the false christs and false prophets spoken of by Gamaliel, the member of the law council, which is the higher Jewish council, as mentioned in Acts 5:36–37.

As for Josephus, the famous Jewish historian who lived in the first Christian century, he lived at the time of the ruin of Jerusalem. He was a judge in the higher Galilee district and was chosen as a translator and a mediator between the Jews and the Roman forces that besieged Jerusalem. Josephus wrote several books still present in our days. In these books, he referred to the appearance of false prophets and false christs. In addition to those mentioned by Josephus, many have appeared across the ages. There is also nothing to stop the team of those false ones from appearing in the future.

3. Wars, Confusion, Rebellion, and Disturbances

This is the third sign. The Lord Jesus informs His disciples that the end would not come before the world was exposed to a chain of wars, rebellions and disturbances. "But when you hear of wars and rumors of wars, do not be troubled; for such things must happen, but the end is not yet. For nation will rise against nation, and kingdom against kingdom" (Mark 13:7–8).

"But when you hear of wars and commotions, do not be terrified; for these things must come to pass first, but the end will not come immediately. Then He said to them, 'Nation will rise against nation, and kingdom against kingdom' (Luke 21:9–10).

In our world, we experience this every day. Since World War II in 1945 and until today, the world has faced numerous wars, rebellions and disturbances in different parts of the world. In this way, Christ's words are literally fulfilled. As we said before, the destruction of Jerusalem is only a miniature image of the end of the world.

Thus, history has recorded to us a horrifying picture of the terrible siege by Roman army of Jerusalem. This was described elaborately by the Jewish historian Josephus, who was a contemporary of this destruction. He said that around 1,100,000 Jews had perished—100,000 perished due to hunger and 97,000 were taken as prisoners of war. The historian underscored phrases that drip blood, such as his saying that the entire hardships and miseries of people, if collected together from the beginning of the entire world, would not be as horrific as that which hit Jerusalem on the day of its destruction! However, the destruction of Jerusalem was not the last of the wars. Rather, it kept being rekindled from time to time, until this day.

Wars, at first, were regional. But today, the world has experienced two "world wars" so far. The world to day continuously fears the eruption of an atomic nuclear warm that could annihilate the entire world. In this way, Christ's words, to Him be the glory, have been fulfilled literally.

4. Natural Disasters

The Lord Jesus, to Him be the glory, said, "There will be great earthquakes in various places, and famines and pestilences; and there will be fearful sights and great signs from heaven" (Luke 21:11). He also says, "There will be earthquakes in various places, and there will be famines and troubles" (Mark 13:8), and "there will be famines, pestilences, and earthquakes in various places" (Matthew 24:7). I think we all hear daily the news of natural disasters, earthquakes, hurricanes, etc.—all that are absolutely destructive.

These disasters demolish tens of thousands in a very short time, and maybe in only a few seconds, as happens in earthquakes. As for the famines that have over swept the world, these caused the death of millions of people and stock animals. The most recent of these is what occurred in Ethiopia. The ghost of starvation still haunts the world and threatens humanity with fearful famine. We also read a great deal about the dangers of drastic floods in India, in China and in other places. All of this reminds us of what the Lord Jesus has said concerning these issues.

5. The Great Apostasy

This sign was mentioned by the Lord Jesus when He was speaking of the hardships that accompany the end of the world: "And then many will be offended, will betray one another, and will hate one another" (Matthew 24:10). Saint Paul the apostle interprets these words plainly saying, "For that Day will not come unless the falling away comes first" (2 Thessalonians 2:3). So, before Christ's Second Coming, the rebellion will take place. Therefore what is meant by the rebellion?

The rebellion or the rejection is of two kinds: the first one is the entire religious rebellion, that is, that man leaves Christianity and diverts to another religion. This would be as a result of persecution and other worldly temptations or sinful lusts. It could also result in converting to current cults such as communism or atheism. The second kind of rebellion means to depart entirely from the spiritual life with God in such a way that the Christian would only bear his name from Christianity. Unfortunately, we find those two kinds of rebellions in millions of victims in our current times. Communism, for instance, fights religion and calls for atheism, which is a dangerous religious rebellion.

Communism has suppressed the Christian pillars in Russia after it used to be the biggest country in the orthodox Christian world. As a result of this, its churches have been transformed to mere museums and most of the Russians have been converted to atheism. Furthermore, many of the western youths today have no religion whatsoever.

As for those who rebel against their spiritual life, these are so many. These are attributed to Christianity only by name! They know nothing about Christianity, and these are the ones Christ, to Him be the glory, meant when speaking of the end of the world, "because lawlessness will abound, the love of many will grow cold" (Matthew 24:12).

5. The Gospel Message Reaches the Entire World

This is the sixth sign for Christ's Second Coming. The Lord Jesus, to Him be the glory, says, "And this gospel of the kingdom will be preached in all the world as a witness to all the nations, and then the end will come" (Matthew 24:14). What do those words mean?

In the interpretation of this verse, the clerical scholars and the scholars of the Holy Book are divided into two groups: one group understands Christ's words in that the

Gospel will spread in the entire world, and thus it will be the golden age for the Christian values to flourish in the world.

As a result, the entire earth will be the Lord's and Christ's, whereas the other group thinks this spreading will only be superficial and apparent, specifically for the judgment day, when the gospel message is not accepted. To prove this, Christ said, "When the Son of Man comes, will He really find faith on the earth?" (Luke 18:8). I personally tend to believe in the second opinion.

6. Signs that Appear in the Sun and the Planets

This is the last sign mentioned by the Lord of glory that precedes His Second Coming. He says, "And there will be signs in the sun, in the moon, and in the stars; and on the earth distress of nations, with perplexity, the sea and the waves roaring; men's hearts failing them from fear and the expectation of those things which are coming on the earth, for the powers of the heavens will be shaken" (Luke 21:25–26). Nowadays we hear of these signs. The solar eclipses are spreading on the surface of the sun, whereas the satellites and spaceships are frequenting space. Quite a number of people have landed on the moon and man has extended his activity to discover the solar planets, which have reached up to Jupiter. In this way, we find that Christ's words are not only fulfilled, but not one letter falls from His words until now. This is in accordance with His divine promise, "Heaven and earth will pass away, but My words will by no means pass away" (Matthew 24:35).

The Preparation for Christ's Second Coming

After we have now been absolutely assured that Christ's Second Coming is an undisputable matter, and that it is a confirmed fact whether we want it or not, accept it or not, are prepared for it or not, let us think together of our situation concerning this crucial and awesome event! How can we be prepared for this advent?

The answer to this question is said by Christ Himself, to Him be the glory. After warning us and manifesting to us clearly the signs for the end of the world and His Second Coming, He said, "Take heed, watch and pray; for you do not know when the time is" (Mark 13:33). From Christ's words, two things are plainly asked of us to do, these are: watchfulness and prayer. We find there is reference to those in Christ's words, to Him be the glory, in Luke 12:43, which is the gospel read in the third service in the midnight prayer. He says, "Blessed is that servant whom his master will find so doing."

Also, He says, "Let your waist be girded and your lamps burning; and you yourselves be like men who wait for their master, when he will return from the wedding, that when he comes and knocks they may open to him immediately. Blessed are those servants whom the master, when he comes, will find watching. Assuredly, I say to you that he will gird himself and have them sit down to eat, and will come and serve them. And if he should come in the second watch, or come in the third watch, and find them so, blessed are those servants" (Luke 12:35).

Therefore, he who wants to be prepared for Christ's Second Coming has to be watchful and pray. There are two types of watchfulness: the physical watchfulness and the spiritual one. Physical watchfulness is well known to us, whereas the spiritual watchfulness means to be watchful in the spirit. Man has to be watchful for the salvation of his soul and should not be careless about it even for a moment. The Lord Jesus, to Him be the glory, cautioned us of this in the parable of grain and the weeds against being sleepy. The adversary sowed weeds among the grain when the people were asleep (Matthew 13:24–28). When a person sleeps concerning the salvation of his soul, the enemy comes and plants in his thoughts and heart whatever he wishes to plant, all of which are corruptive and cause corruption.

There is a beautiful story of two martyrs, a husband and a young wife. They were watchful when embracing death. The husband was the deacon Timothy in Upper Egypt, in a small village, and his young wife, Mora, was only sixteen. Soon after their marriage, the governor Arianus ordered the arrest of this deacon who kept the holy books of the church. The governor tortured this deacon so he would hand the books over to him so that he could burn them. This was to follow and carry out the order given by the despot Diocletian in 303 AD. The deacon refused to comply. Some of his courtiers informed the governor that the deacon had married a young girl a few days ago and that undoubtedly the deacon would yield to the governor if he brought the wife to lure him so that his stubbornness might yield. The governor, therefore, brought the wife and ordered her to put her best clothes on, to wear perfume and to adorn herself so she would make her husband submit and yield. When Mora came, the husband warned her of listening to the governor's wishes and informed her that suffering for Christ's sake is the goal of every Christian. As soon as she heard this, her heart opened up and she desired to suffer for Christ's name. She therefore declared her faith and joined her husband in being tortured without flinching. The governor finally ordered them to be put to death by crucifying them. They greatly rejoiced in this. On their way to being crucified they agreed together not to go to sleep on the cross, lest Christ comes and finds them asleep! Can you imagine, dear friends, how watchful the first Christians were? Even when embracing death, they were careful to be watchful.

The first Christian generations and the believers at that time lived in constant expectation of the Lord's coming. The wonderful greeting they saluted each other with was "Maranatha" (1 Corinthians 16:22), which is an Aramaic phrase that means, "Come, O Lord." This applies identically to the words said by Saint John in the book of Revelation, which is the last book in the entire Holy Bible, "Amen. Even so, come, Lord Jesus!" (22:20).

Christ's Millennium Reign

Some of you may have heard of what is called Christ's millennium reign. This means that Christ will come and rule for a thousand years on earth and will reign physically and materialistically. Those who call for this concept say that those thousand years will have peace and prosperity throughout the world. There would be no wars, to the extent that the wolf will be shepherded with the lamb and that the fighting devices of death will be transformed to devices for agriculture and harvesting. Where did people bring this idea from?

Some have based their concept on what is mentioned in the book of Revelation 20:1–10 when compared to what was mentioned in Isaiah 2:4 and Micah 4:3. "Then I saw an angel coming down from heaven, having the key to the bottomless pit and a great chain in his hand. He laid hold of the dragon, that serpent of old, who is the Devil and Satan, and bound him for a thousand years; and he cast him into the bottomless pit, and shut him up, and set a seal on him, so that he should deceive the nations no more till the thousand years were finished. But after these things he must be released for a little while. And I saw thrones, and they sat on them, and judgment was committed to them. Then I saw the souls of those who had been beheaded for their witness to Jesus and for the word of God, who had not worshiped the beast or his image, and had not received his mark on their foreheads or on their hands. And they lived and reigned with Christ for a thousand years. But the rest of the dead did not live again until the thousand years were finished. This is the first resurrection. Blessed and holy is he who has part in the first resurrection. Over such the second death has no power, but they shall be priests of God and of Christ, and shall reign with Him a thousand years. Now when the thousand years have expired, Satan will be released from his prison and will go out to deceive the nations which are in the four corners of the earth, Gog and Magog, to gather them together to battle, whose number is as the sand of the sea. They went up on the breadth of the earth and surrounded the camp of saints and the beloved city. And fire came down from God out of heaven and devoured them. The devil, who deceived them, was cast into the lake of fire and brimstone where the beast and the false prophet are. And they will be tormented day and night forever and ever."

When we speak of the millennium reign, we are naturally speaking from the opinion and the creed angle of the Coptic Orthodox Church. Concerning this issue, there are two opinions that have appeared in the history of the first church.

The first opinion: This says that Christ rules the earth for a thousand years that are full of welfare and peace, a reign of real materialism. This opinion is not a recent one; rather, it came to be since the olden times at the dawn of Christianity. Those of this opinion were Jewish conquerors who were actually a group of the Jews who believed in Christ and who called for the necessity of keeping some of the Jewish habits.

These victorious Jews, or more correctly, the Christian Jews, wearied the first church in its apostolic age a great deal, particularly Saint Paul the apostle. Because of them, the father apostles convened a church assembly in the city of Jerusalem around the year 50 AD. They decided not to adhere to the old Jewish law (Acts 15:1–29). The idea of the millennium reign of Christ is the outcome of these victorious Jews, or the Christian Jews. The Jews have not accepted Christ because they found Him to be so humble that He does not shout out and no one in the street could hear His voice. He would not strike a reed and a smoked candle He does not blow out. Such a Christ was not appropriate for the Jewish reaction and He did not agree with the picture they drew of Christ deep inside of them. They wanted a strong and fearful Christ, a revered king, a Christ who would free them politically from the Roman bondage which occupied their land and a Christ who would bring for them a wide dominion and bring back David's religious kingdom.

But as for the Christ who came, He tried to teach the Jews that the real bondage is not their bondage to the Romans, but it was rather their bondage to sin. The true freedom was for man to be released from the bondage of sin. This was Christ's mission who came to release man from the chains of his sin (John 8:34, 36). These words did not please the Jews and did not satisfy their desires to domineer and authorize. They wanted a Christ similar to Samson the valiant one, who would add kingdoms, cities and lands to their own possessions. The idea of possessions prevailed over them. Christ, according to their understanding, would come out of David's lineage, biologically speaking, so He would bring back David's kingdom and retrieve it as it used to be. Their hope was for a Christ who would come and reign. Concerning this we say: we cannot understand the establishment of Israel at the present time except within this framework. This is a country established having authority over its neighbors, and if possible, over the entire world.

That Christ should come for a spiritual mission and that He would not come again except for judgment is something they did not hope for or take into account. In this way, we find that the well based idea of the dominant kingdom is in the depths of the Jews' minds. Even after their being converted to Christianity, we find it floating on the surface of their thoughts. Thus, they are trying to spread the idea of the millennium reign for Christ. In their opinion, Christ will come and will reign for a thousand years. In this way, their hopes, their thoughts and their old Jewish imagination will be fulfilled. Unfortunately, we find this corrupt creed that calls for the millennium reign, the materialistic one for Christ, penetrating some Christian sects, beginning from the sixteenth century with the appearance of Protestantism in Europe. Soon enough, the creed spread in America as well. We find this in the sect of the Seventh Day Adventists (Christ is coming Adventists) as well as Jehovah's witnesses who made this their greatest and their foremost creed. They began to set specific times for Christ's coming and the beginning of His millennium reign. Of course, all of the set dates they specified were false and were mocked by everyone!

The second opinion in the issue of the millennium reign for Christ is the opinion of our straightforward church in which we believe, as well as all the apostolic churches and the great church fathers. The conclusion for this opinion is that Christ's reign is actually a spiritual one, as He said to Pontius Pilate, "My kingdom is not of this world" (John 18:36). The Lord Jesus, in the Lord's prayer, has taught us to pray like this, "Hallowed be Thy name, Thy kingdom come."

The meaning of "Thy kingdom come" is, "Come, O Lord reign over my heart, and reign over people's hearts. Therefore this kingdom is a spiritual one. Thus we can see the Lord Jesus confirming this meaning more than once, and so He says, "for indeed, the kingdom of God is within you" (Luke 17:21). From here we can say that now we are in the reign of the thousand years mentioned in the book of Revelation. Since the day Christ made the salvation for the world, everyone who believes in Him is in the millennium reign. Of course, there are many verses that are related to this topic that could be elaborated on. Actually, the issue of the millennium reign needs a special book and long and inclusive research. We think it enough here to speak of it that much.

But the period of a thousand years is not exactly a thousand years in time. Saint Peter the apostle says, "But, beloved, do not forget this one thing, that with the Lord one day is a thousand years, and a thousand years as one day" (2 Peter 3:8). All the numbers mentioned in the book of Revelation are symbolic numbers. One of the matters that distinguish the millennium reign is the presence of peace.

We thank God we are blessed with this peace, for Christ is our peace (Ephesians 2:14). In the Gregorian Liturgy, the priest says, addressing Christ, the Son of God, "You...became for us a Mediator with the Father, and the middle wall You have broken down, and the old enmity You have abolished. You have reconciled the earthly with the heavenly, and have made the two into one."

In the Serbian fraction, the priest prays, saying, "Christ has confirmed with the blood of His cross, and has unified and reconciled the heavenly with the earthly, and the nation with the nations, and the soul with the body." As for the words that one of the landmarks of the thousand years is that Satan will be chained, this is what is actually happening, because Satan is bounded now. If Satan had been released of every bond, our disasters would have been so many and so dangerous.

But someone may say, "If Satan is chained, then from where is the evil that fills the world today, and that fills so many millions of people?" We answer and say, the fact that Satan is chained cannot be doubted. He has been chained by the cross, and to prove this, are the words of Christ Himself in John 12:31, "Now the ruler of this world will be cast out."

The ruler of this world is Satan. This Christ also said about him, "For the ruler of this world is coming, and he has nothing in Me" (John 14:30). Our teacher Saint Paul the apostle says about Christ, "Having wiped out the handwriting of requirements that was against us, which was contrary to us. And He has taken it out of the way, having nailed it to the cross. Having disarmed principalities and powers, He made a public spectacle of them, triumphing over them in it" (Colossians 2:14–15). Satan has fallen and has been done away with, and this is why the Lord Jesus said, "Behold, I give you the authority to trample on serpents and scorpions, and over all the power of the enemy, and nothing shall by any means hurt you" (Luke 10:19). We shall tread on every power of the enemy, and nothing will ever hurt us. How can the believer have this right when the devil is unchained?

Let us refer to the question above, which is, if Satan is bound, then how can this evil in the world be explained? Actually Satan is chained, now, but at the present time, he is playing the role of the tempter, or the deceiver of lust and passion. We can liken Satan's role to a fearful and strong person who is tied by a chain.

Despite his chains, he is able to do certain movements, and is threatening to the close ones to him. He is as the lion when in his iron cage in the zoo, if he roars all those of tender hearts shake in spite of the fact that he is in an iron cage! Saint Peter the Apostle says, "Your adversary the devil walks about like a roaring lion, seeking whom he may devour. Resist him, steadfast in the faith" (1 Peter 5:8–9).

By meditating on this verse, it is clear to us that Satan is chained, for the apostle says he is as a roaring lion. We know that the lion does not roar or prowl on any victim unless he feels hungry, and thus he expresses his hunger by roaring. As soon as the other animals in the jungle hear the lion roaring, they flee away from his face. If Satan had not been chained by God's command, he would have devoured his prey at once. But he is chained, and thus he only roars so as to frighten those weak souls, the unrepentant ones. Then they crack and fall into sin due to their fear, despite the fact that he is chained. Now Satan is chained, and he has no authority over us at all.

For God has given us the authority to tread upon him and to crush him. "But as many as received Him, to them He gave the right to become children of God" (John 1:12). In this way we can confirm and say that every time we fall into sin, we are actually responding to Satan's temptation, though he is chained. It is sad indeed to hear that someone tries to justify his fall by saying that Satan has tricked him!

Is not this a confession of his foolishness? Satan is like a lion caged in the zoo. If someone draws close to him, and stretches out his hand inside the cage, then the lion will not hesitate to pounce on this stretched out hand and will devour it at once. Naturally, the mistake is not that of the lion in his cage, but rather it is the mistake of the person who came forward and stretched his hand inside the cage! Likewise is the chained devil; he will not be able to reach out to any believer who is far away from him and from the dangerous area around him. If someone feels like intruding on the lion's den, and wallow in sin, then Satan will be quick enough to devour him up! The evil in the world is a result of fear, little faith, and throwing oneself into Satan's embrace, the father of every sin!

The First and the Second Resurrections

One of the issues we face is the verse, "But the rest of the dead did not live again until the thousand years were finished. This is the first resurrection. Blessed and holy is he who has part in the first resurrection. Over such the second death has no power" (Revelations 20:1–10). There are two resurrections, a first one and a second one. What is the first resurrection, and what is the second one? In other words, what are the first death and the second one?

1. The First Resurrection

He means the spiritual resurrection from the spiritual death; for we were dead in sin and iniquity (Ephesians

2:1). By our acceptance of Christ, and by our repentance, we are raised from this spiritual death. There are endless verses that prove this. This is why the Lord Jesus said to His apostles, "Most assuredly, I say to you, he who believes in Me, the works that I do he will do also; and greater works that these he will do" (John 14:12). This is amazing indeed! How can man do greater works than what Christ did?

To understand these difficult words, we ask: "What are the greatest works Christ did?" Undoubtedly, it is the raising of the dead. What is greater than the raising of the dead, which the believer in Christ can perform? The fathers say the raising of the spiritually dead is greater than the raising of the physically dead. The first resurrection mentioned in the book of Revelation is the spiritual resurrection from the spiritual death, that is, the faith in Christ, in repentance, the partnership with Him and in Him.

Our teacher Saint Paul the apostle says, "And [God] raised us up together, and made us sit together in the heavenly places in Christ Jesus" (Ephesians 2:6). This is the first resurrection in the Christian understanding. Thus we can hear the Lord Jesus, to Him be the glory, say when raising Lazarus from the dead, "I am the resurrection and the life. He who believes in Me, though he may die, he shall live. And whoever lives and believes in Me shall never die" (John 11:25–26). Naturally, Christ means here the spiritual death. The Lord confirms this meaning also when He says, "Most assuredly, I say to you, the hour is coming, and now is, when the dead will hear the voice of the Son of God; and those who hear will live" (John

5:25). The meaning of "the dead" here, is the spiritually dead, that is, sinners. The evidence referring to this is "and now is" because when He said these words no one was raised from among the dead!

2. The Second Resurrection

This is the resurrection of the bodies after the end of times, for the general judgment. "The hour is coming in which all who are in the graves will hear His voice and come forth—those who have done good, to the resurrection of life, and those who have done evil, to the resurrection of condemnation" (John 5:28–29). Therefore, the first resurrection is the spiritual one, whereas the second one is that of the bodies for the judgment. The first death is the death of sin, and the second death is that of the body, that will be resurrected the second time for judgment.

We have learned from the above and according to our church teaching that we are now living in this millennium for Christ. Christ reigns now in the believers and over them. Christ's reign mentioned in the book of Revelation is actually what the Christian church lives now with Christ in heaven and on earth in the blessing of His kingdom. Concerning this, Saint Augustine says, "There will be no Christ's coming before His final appearance for judgment, because His coming is actually happening now in the church and in our bodies. Christ's millennium reign has actually begun on earth, and Christ Himself is in the church, and the saints are ruling now."

The End of the World and Christ's Second Coming

After speaking of the signs for Christ's Second Coming, let us meditate together on the end of the world and Christ's Second Coming. This issue has been mentioned in detail in Matthew 24 and 25. Based on our study of this, we can deduce the following facts about the end of the world:

The sun will be darkened and the moon will not give its light. This goes in accordance with the scientific theory that says the moon takes its light from the sun. Also, the starts will fall from heaven and the powers of heaven will be shaken.

The Son of Man's sign will appear in the sky, and this sign is the cross (Matthew 24:30). Christ will come on the clouds in great power and glory, (Matthew 24:30, Luke 21:27, 1 Thessalonians 4:17)

With the archangel's trumpet, he gathers everyone for judgment. All the dead will rise, in whatever death they died. "For the Lord Himself will descend from heaven with a cry of command, with the archangel's call and with the sound of the trumpet of God. And the dead in Christ will rise first" (1 Thessalonians 4:16).

The dead in Christ will rise first, and this is the second resurrection (1 Thessalonians 4:16). After this, the living who have not yet died, will change, and they will all meet the Lord on the clouds (4:17).

The Judgment: All will stand before Christ for the

judgment (Matthew 25:31–46). The dead will rise, not to rule with Christ for a thousand years, as some assume, but rather, for everyone to stand before Christ for the judgment. How I wish to give you a detailed picture of the judgment. Please review Saint Matthew's gospel, Chapter 25, so you may know how Christ will speak and how He will judge both the righteous and the wicked ones. Meditate with me on some of what is mentioned in this beautiful chapter.

"When the Son of Man comes in His glory, and all the holy angels with Him, then He will sit on the throne of His glory. All the nations will be gathered before Him, and He will separate them one from another, as a shepherd divides his sheep from the goats. And He will set the sheep on His right hand, but the goats on the left. Then the King will say to those on His right hand, 'Come, you blessed of My Father, inherit the kingdom prepared for you form the foundation of the world: for I was hungry and you gave Me food; I was thirsty and you gave Me drink; I was a stranger and you took Me in; I was naked and you clothed Me; I was sick and you visited Me; I was in prison and you came to Me.' Then the righteous will answer Him, saying, 'Lord, when did we see You hungry and feed You, or thirsty and give You drink?' And the king will answer and say to them, 'Assuredly, I say to you, inasmuch as you did it to one of the least of these My brethren, you did it to Me.'"

The "least of these My brethren" are our poor brethren. The issue needs a long struggle and constant toil in the spiritual life. But once a person reaches there, he forgets all his toil to the extent that he tells the Lord Jesus, 'When did I do this?' He has forgotten all the toil, for God will wipe every tear of our eyes. Saint Peter the apostle says, "For so an entrance will be supplied to you abundantly into the everlasting kingdom of our Lord and Savior Jesus Christ" (2 Peter 1:11). Yes, He will richly provide, that is, there is a precious chance to enter heaven. So, do you want to enter heaven? Blessed is the man whose eagerness is to go there. But as for those ones on the left, they will hear terrible things, "Depart from Me, you cursed, into the everlasting fire prepared for the devil and his angels: for I was hungry and you gave Me no food; I was thirsty and you gave Me no drink; I was a stranger and you did not take Me in, naked and you did not clothe Me, sick and in prison and you did not visit Me.' Then they also will answer, 'Lord, when...?' Then He will answer them, saying, 'Assuredly, I say to you, inasmuch as you did not do it to one of the least of these, you did not do it to Me.' And these will go away into everlasting punishment, but the righteous into eternal life" (Matthew 25:41–46).

But we have to note an important fact, which is that hunger is not merely the hunger for bread, but there is a far worse and more severe hunger, which is that hunger for the Word of God and the thirst for salvation.

The naked is not only meant to have no clothes on, but the nakedness of something else, for Adam and Eve when they fell into sin, they felt that they were naked. Moreover, the Prodigal Son, when he returned to his father in regret, he was naked because he was in rags. This is why we find the father commanding the servants to clothe him in the best garment. This means that if we are able to bring any person who is from God back to Christ, then we are actually satisfying him with God's word, allowing him to drink of Christ's love and clothing him with the garment of righteousness, faith and Christian virtues. I wish we could understand these sayings in this framework!

The Heavenly Wedding

After the judgment, the believers go in a wedding procession to the Bridegroom, or to the heavenly Seal of circumcision, our Lord Jesus Christ. We all are engaged to Him, men and women, boys and girls, as St. Paul the Apostle says, "For I have betrothed you to one husband" (2 Corinthians 11:2).

The Lord Jesus compared the heavenly kingdom to a wedding where there are virgins who took their lamps and went out to meet the groom (Matthew 25:1–13). All the souls are engaged to Christ and He alone is the Groom, whereas all of us compose the bride. With God's will, all of us will go to the procession to our heavenly Groom. This is in absolute love in fulfillment to the Lord's words in John 17:26: "That the love with which You loved Me may be in them, and I in them.

Dear brethren, we are eagerly looking forward to these moments that will surely come to be. We speak in hearts full of hope and with hearts full of love, trust and faith in our Lord Jesus Christ, for He has loved us for no reason and has freely saved us. We thank Him for His blessings that have overcome us, and we ask Him to keep us in the unity of the Spirit. May He grant us the life of faith, love and hope. May He give us the life of holy partnership with Him.

We ask our God that He does not allow anyone to perish, we the members of the Church on earth, so we may also be with Him around the throne of His heavenly grace in heaven. We ask Him to forgive us our sins and to write our names in the Book of Life, so that we may have a share and inheritance with Him in the heavenly Jerusalem. Amen.